Location Is (Still) Everything

Location Is (Still) Everything

The Surprising Influence of the Real
World on How We Search, Shop, and
Sell in the Virtual One

DAVID R. BELL

amazonpublishing

Published by Amazon Publishing, Seattle

www.apub.com

Amazon, the Amazon logo and Amazon Publishing are trademarks of Amazon.com, Inc. or its affiliates.

ISBN-13 (paperback): 9781477801178

Cover design by Faceout Studio, Charles Brock
Cover image © Shutterstock
Author photograph © Tommy Leonardi

To Anne and Trevor
Model parents in the real world and the virtual one as well

CONTENTS

Location Is (Still) Everything

The Surprising Influence of the Real World
on How We Search, Shop, and Sell
in the Virtual One

T he TV was on in the background.

"He's not the Messiah, he's a very naughty boy!" Brian's mom is half shouting, half shrieking to the hordes who've been following her son around in Monty Python's *Life of Brian,* after mixing him up with someone rather more important.

Distracted, I took a look at the *Daily Mail* on my iPad.

The leader of the free world, it seems, has a slightly different problem. President Barack Obama, unlike Brian, is certainly a legitimate leader, but he has been crowned the "King of the Fake Twitter Followers" for having more than 19.5 million followers who don't actually exist.[1]

This past summer I'd been following another Bryan (Cranston) myself, in the form of Walter White, the central character in the hit TV show *Breaking Bad.* Walter was mentioned on Twitter nearly 200,000 times during the screening of the show's finale in late September, and a disproportionate number came from real-world locations on the coasts

---

1 David Martosko, "Barack Obama Is Political King of the Fake Twitter Followers, with More Than 19.5 Million Online Fans Who Don't Really Exist," *Daily Mail,* September 24, 2013, www.dailymail.co.uk/news/article-2430875/Barack-Obama-19-5m-fake-Twitter-followers .html.

of the United States. After the East Coast showing began, the tweets peaked at over 22,000 per minute![2]

I looked around my apartment.

I needed to unpack those Soap.com and Harrys.com boxes containing my household supplies and razors, respectively. I'd had them delivered to work, so they'd been sitting in the marketing department at Wharton for a few days. Perhaps due to the striking packaging, some of my colleagues were now placing orders too. I wondered if there would be some ripple effect to their friends and neighbors as well.

In five days I was scheduled to travel to Tyler, Texas, and if I was going to catch the New Zealand All Blacks in their next big rugby game, I'd have to pipe the live feed from StreamHunter.eu and would probably join the commentary on Rugby365.com. There aren't too many real-world rugby fans in Tyler, so the virtual-world community was my way out. I then had a fleeting thought: Was all this virtual-world connectivity making me too insular in my interests? What real-world delights in Tyler would I miss as a result?

It was getting late, but I needed to write a bit, so I reflected on a couple of my recent findings in a research project that had really intrigued me. One of my coauthors, Jeonghye Choi, and I had found that Diapers.com, a seller of baby products, had a dramatically *higher* demand for its services in locations where there were proportionally *fewer* households, percentagewise, with young children. Real-world sellers in these locations weren't too fussed about catering to these "minority" customers. So a virtual-world seller like Diapers.com was a godsend for these people.

Another coauthor, Jae Young Lee, and I had also just found that within real-world communities with high levels of trust and interaction, information about a virtual-world seller specializing in men's apparel, Bonobos.com, shared by existing customers was more believable to potential customers. In fact, this real-world information transmission was driving a lot of the virtual-world sales.

Finally, I decided to turn in, but something in the *New York Times* caught my eye: "To Catch Up, Walmart Moves to Amazon Turf"—and a

---

2 Julia Boorstin, "Why and How the 'Breaking Bad' Finale Broke Records," Media Money, CNBC, September 30, 2013, www.cnbc.com/id/101074132. See also Sara Morrison "'Breaking Bad' Finale . . . By the Tweets (Updated)," tv.yahoo.com/news/breaking-bad-finale-tweets-170345402.html.

(virtual) light went off before I flicked the real one down.[3] The real and the virtual worlds are coming together in exciting ways, and there is a story to be told about why and how this is happening.

For as long as we've had trade and commerce, much of the underlying economics has been explained by location. *Déjà vu!* It startled me how much this remains true in the borderless, and often anonymous, virtual world. It became clear to me that night that it isn't simply *who* you and I are that's important for the answers but also *where* we are. Even in the virtual world, it's *still* all about "location, location, location." Furthermore, virtual-world sellers of products and content have very predictable demand patterns—once you understand where the target customers are.

The Real World and the Virtual World

The voice-over that introduces *Star Trek* states that space is the "final frontier." It is out there, vast and different from everything we are used to on Earth. Similarly, the Internet and its related technologies give us access to incredible new worlds of products and information. Only a few short years ago, these things were inaccessible and perhaps even beyond comprehension.

Since the Internet is a transformative technology, it's obviously worth knowing how best to make use of what it offers. It can improve the way you spend your money, make your job more interesting (or even eliminate it!), transform entire industries, and connect you with others the world over. More broadly, it plays a key role in everything from the organic discovery of talented musicians like Lorde (the pop star from Devonport, New Zealand) to the trajectory of important political and cultural events like the Arab Spring, to why I stopped buying razors in the supermarket and get them directly from Harrys.com.

So while it's one thing to use the Internet (most of us do), it's another to understand how it might help, hurt, or alter our individual and

---

3 Claire Cain Miller and Stephanie Clifford, "To Catch Up, Walmart Moves to Amazon Turf," *New York Times*, October 19, 2013, www.nytimes.com/2013/10/20/technology/to-catch-up-walmart-moves-to-amazon-turf.html?_r=0&adxnnl=1&adxnnlx=1382332994-oowfCO eqN2362ZziCu9DvA.

collective lives. In fact, the impact it is having on our daily lives and on commerce all over the world exceeds anything that has preceded it. This includes momentous inventions such as the internal combustion engine and the printing press.

The sheer scale of the e-commerce sector in the economy gives some perspective as well. According to the most recent US Census e-commerce reports, about $5.5 trillion changes hands online versus about $19 trillion offline.[4] The rate of growth of e-commerce over the last decade exceeds 125 percent (more than four times the "nominal" rate for offline commerce). Among the four key sectors of the economy in general, manufacturing, wholesale, retail, and services, retail growth is the most explosive, exceeding 220 percent over the last decade.

What we are finding is that the way we use the *virtual world* of the Internet—for commerce and for information—is dictated to a large extent by the *physical world* that each of us resides in. This influence is pervasive, and sometimes counterintuitive, with implications for our lives in both worlds.

There is a key implication that I will explore throughout this book: if you and I live under different physical circumstances and in different physical environments, we will use the virtual world very differently—even if we are very similar people in terms of our ages, incomes, education levels, and so on. We'll shop differently, search differently, and won't be equally attractive to sellers.

So if we want to make sense of how we use the virtual world, we need to have a framework for understanding the different influences of the real world on how we shop, search, and sell online.

We'll also need to think about what people want (e.g., the desire to get things done quickly, to have access to reliable information, and to be able to find great deals on things they'd like to have) and what motivates these desires. Sometimes people want to be transparent—or at least we want others to be. At other times, we'd rather be anonymous.

If we're fully cognizant of these fundamental drivers of behavior, we can develop usable insights into the conditions under which the virtual

---

4   United States Census Bureau, "E-Stats," United States Department of Commerce, Economics and Statistics Administration, May 23, 2013, www.census.gov//econ/estats/2011reportfinal .pdf.

world enhances, supplants, augments, or replaces what we do in the real one.

This knowledge is not only interesting in its own right (share it and you'll be more popular at cocktail parties), but it is also practical for those of us who want to create new Internet businesses, turbocharge existing ones, or just better understand what these new technologies mean for us.

Young, wealthy, and well-educated citizens are the most active in the virtual world. This reflects the so-called digital divide, or the discrepancy between those who have access to the Internet and those who do not. Within a country, individuals who live in rural areas, or those with lower educational attainment and less income, tend to use the Internet less. Beyond this basic discrepancy in access, people in some locations are far more apt to shop online than those in others. Certain kinds of individuals use the Internet to "liberate themselves" from their lack of offline options.

Why are these things so?

The value of reviews and information depends a lot on from where (and not just from whom) they come from. Some sites generate almost all their traffic from particular locations. Buyers in online auctions prefer to deal with sellers who live close to them. When we shop offline, the distance that we need to travel to reach sellers always matters for our choices, but as I explain later, we're even less willing to travel further when we're searching for sellers on our mobile devices.

What's behind these and other effects of the physical world on how we shop, sell, and search in the virtual world?

That's what this book is all about.

Location, as it turns out, is (still) everything.

First Things First—Physical Location Before the Virtual One

In the story of the chicken and the egg, it's hard to tell which came first. Not so with the physical and virtual worlds. The physical world, including the cities and many of the communities that we inhabit, has been around for a while. You've no doubt put some thought into where you're currently living.

Your station in the real world is, in large part, a choice.

It's unlikely that you simply fell into the flat, town house, apartment, or suburban McMansion that you currently live in. There probably are good reasons behind the housing choices that you've made. The same goes for your choice of city.[5] And for the company that you keep, including friends, acquaintances, and the people you follow online.

These decisions are not like the "decision" that occurred just prior to the Colgate toothpaste falling into your shopping cart. They are, for the most part, and for most of us, carefully considered decisions. They have a long shelf life.

That's good news for this book.

It means that the relationships that exist between our *physical-world locations* and our *virtual-world behaviors* will be robust. They'll be pretty stable and quite predictable. Indeed, the very idea that your circumstances in the physical world shape your behavior in the virtual world may seem rather obvious after you've seen the reasons why. (Good and lasting ideas always seem intuitive once you have the means to appreciate them.)

Nevertheless, elaboration is required because many of the nuanced observations that support this central idea are not obvious. So, too, are the implications for what this means for consumers, for entrepreneurs, for investors, for regulators, and really, for all of us.

"Newton Got Beaned by the Apple Good"

Even if you didn't pay much attention to science lessons in high school, you probably still have a good idea of what Newton discovered. When the apple (literally) dropped, Newton was hit with the concept of gravity. A parallel concept, the "theory of (commercial) gravity" is central to, and very important for, this book.

Here's why.

Gravitational pull is the reason I'd be better off taking the elevator

---

5   Although people do of course end up in cities they don't seem to like a whole lot. The derisive and provocative site phillysucks.com is a testament to some Philadelphians' dissatisfaction with their city. If you're curious about people's negative reactions to *your* city, just go to Google and type, "Why is [your city] so . . ." and see what comes up.

in my apartment building rather than the "shortcut" of jumping out the window onto the street. Similarly, the real world imposes gravitylike forces and other frictions on all of us as we search, shop, and sell.[6] The practical nuances are a bit different from those exerted by the Earth's physical gravity, but the principle at work is very comparable.

Say that I want a cold beer to combat the oppressive Philadelphia summer heat (I do). Consider too that I'm a lousy planner (I am) and that my fridge is barren (it is). This means that I've got to get up out of my chair and head to the store.

The liquor stores that are closer to me exert more "pull" over me. Other stores are simply too far away and will have no (gravitational) pull.

I like beer, but I am not driving to Wilmington, Delaware, to get it!

However, before I visit *any* of the stores that have enough "pull" over me to get me in the door, I won't know exactly what they have in stock or how much I'll have to pay. I usually can't figure that out until I get to the stores and start scanning the shelves. On top of all this, if it's a Sunday, then because of where I live (Philadelphia), all of the liquor stores will be closed.

So there you have it. The real world is throwing a few obstacles in front of me before I get that cold ale. I need to transport myself to a store; I don't quite know what I'll have to pay (or sometimes even whether I am getting ripped off by my local proprietor); and, if my thirst coincides with a particular day of the week, I am in deep trouble.

Why am I bringing all of this up?

Well, it's often said that the Internet and its related technologies "reduce frictions" and therefore "make the world flat."[7] The virtual world sits there above us (or perhaps below), and it can be accessed at any time, anywhere, by anybody. This is an appealing idea, but it's not quite right.

---

6   The word "friction" is a good one. Economists like it a lot because it conveys the idea that searching and shopping for goods and services takes effort and involves "resistance." Hence, it's a good way to think about what is going on when we have difficulty getting the products and information that we want in real markets.

7   A fascinating piece by Richard Florida from George Mason University highlights this point from another angle. He shows in map form that there are enormous "spikes" of creativity and talent in certain cities around the world (as measured by, say, the number of patents and scientific citations). See "The World Is Spiky," *Atlantic Monthly*, October 2005, 48–51, www .theatlantic.com/past/docs/images/issues/200510/world-is-spiky.pdf.

For starters, it's only *half* true.

Now the first part is certainly correct. Frictions get reduced and, in some cases, are practically eliminated in the virtual world (we will see this in detail in chapter 2). And it's definitely true that many of us now have access to products and information, largely independent of the physical world that we inhabit.

The second part, however, is not true.

Even though the Internet has the *potential* to make the real world flat,[8] this potential is not always realized, and for a very good reason. As long as we still live in the real world, its gravity and frictions will still impact the choices we make there. And, because they impact our choices, they will also affect the *relative* attractiveness of things available online. The real-world landscape we live in even influences our motivations to utilize the virtual world in the first place.

Anyone in the United States (or even the world) *could*, for example, go to Bonobos.com and buy a pair of comfortable and stylish pants. (In fact, I encourage any male aged roughly twenty to forty-five who has not already done so to visit the site; "pantsformation" awaits!) But *the chance that a specific individual actually visits the site depends a lot on where he or she lives.*

The presence of local stores, as well as that of trendy and friendly neighbors who may have already tried the product, or who have endorsed it, will play a role in this decision. So too will the prices charged by the local stores, their selections, and whether or not they add sales tax to the final price.

Linking the Real World and the Virtual World

So, the *virtual world* of the Internet— with its products and information—sits there, offering us all kinds of stuff. And, importantly for our purposes, it offers us things (almost) *regardless* of where we live. Pretty much wherever we are, we can get anything we want.

In theory, products and information can traverse the world very

---

8   If you're interested in more details, see Frances Cairncross, *The Death of Distance: How the Communication Revolution Will Change Our Lives* (Boston: Harvard Business School Press, 2001).

easily via the Internet. For example, I can be anywhere in the United States (or even the world) and follow @fancyckn's missives on Twitter. Whether I live in Los Angeles or Iowa City, I can buy a pair of stylish Warby Parker glasses for $95. I have 24-7 access to flights on the United Airlines app, and the prices and flights available are the same at any time, regardless of where I happen to be.

So wherever I am, the virtual world doesn't really change at all. Conversely, the *real world* varies dramatically from one location to the next, in terms of products, information, and entertainment available offline. Depending on where I live, I will have more or less time to spend on social media sites, or even more or less inclination to use them. I'll have more or less need to shop online and be more or less willing to interact with others in either world. Additionally, my local options for eyewear (and even the need to be stylish or trendy) change as I head from place to place.

So, let's get back to what's flat and what's not. Even my desire to leave once in a while and book a United Airlines flight out of my hometown depends a lot on where I call home to begin with.

The virtual world *is* flat in terms of the opportunity that it delivers to all of us, but it *is not* flat in the way that we use it.

And the reason is simple.

Because the way we use it to search, shop, and sell depends on where we live in the *real world,* which is anything but flat.

My own personal journey through the real world has shaped the way I think about the virtual world. And where I currently live most of the time (Philadelphia) causes me to use the Internet differently than I have when I've lived elsewhere (e.g., Los Angeles or New York City).

Adventures in the Real and Virtual Worlds

I grew up in a place famous for, among other things, a large sheep-to-person ratio. In Invercargill, New Zealand, during the late 1970s and early 1980s, the real world was simple and quite pleasant, but somewhat limited in its offerings.

I was fascinated by the seemingly endless variation in the real world that I saw not only in my own country when my family vacationed in

Christchurch and when we ultimately moved to Auckland, but also on television. There I saw the gray skies of London in *EastEnders*, the sunny open highways of Los Angeles in *L.A. Law*, and the urban intricacy of the Bay Area in *The Streets of San Francisco*. At that time, little did I know that I'd visit all of those places, and that I'd even do a bit of real- and virtual-world shopping and searching in each. (I haven't done any selling in these places as of yet, though.)

As a PhD student at the Stanford Graduate School of Business in the mid-1990s, I was drawn to study two very basic human activities, shopping and consuming. (Unfortunately, as a PhD student, I had neither the time nor the money for either activity!)

It was at Stanford that I learned about Reilly's law of retail gravitation, which describes in simple terms how you and I as consumers decide where to buy the goods and services that we consume. When William J. Reilly published this idea in 1931, there was, of course, no virtual world of the Internet. But his idea—that your choice to visit "location A" over "location B" as a place to shop depends on the relative populations of those two places and their relative distances from you—is still a powerful one.[9] The bigger that a place is, the more attractive it will be for shopping (it will have a greater selection of products and more favorable prices), and the farther away it is, the less attractive it will be (it will have less pull).

---

9 Specifically, the retail gravity model gives us a simple way of calculating the point at which a shopper is indifferent to the choice of shopping in either location A or location B. (Jean-Paul Rodrigue, PhD, of Hofstra University has a nice illustration available at http://people .hofstra.edu/geotrans/eng/methods/reillylaw.html.) If city A and city B are 75km apart, then a naive answer would be that someone living at the halfway point (37.5km) is indifferent between visiting either one. However, since more populous cities have more stuff, we need to take that into account. This leads to the following formula: Indifference Point Between City A and City B =

$$\frac{D}{1 + \sqrt{P_A/P_B}}$$

where D is the distance between the cities (75km in the example) and P_A and P_B are the populations of cities A and B. If we assume them to be 250,000 and 100,000 respectively, then a shopper located 45.9 km from city A and 29.1km from city B would be indifferent to the two.

This core framework is a very good starting point for trying to figure out how offline options for selling, searching, and shopping impact our online options for doing the same thing. If "big places" (that is, shopping options with attractive pricing and lots of variety) are far from you, then the offline world has little pull over your behavior, making the online world quite attractive.

Since I'd already been studying shopping and consuming in the offline world as a student, I was able to make this connection a few years later when, as a faculty member at the Wharton School of the University of Pennsylvania, I was suddenly confronted with the new and exciting world of the Internet.

"Internet 1.0" was bubbling right along when I arrived at Wharton. In the late 1990s and early 2000s, I watched with great amazement as new businesses like Pets.com (pet supplies), Webvan.com (groceries), and Kozmo.com (delivery) came and went. My curiosity was piqued, and I was determined to try to understand what was driving these opportunities, the spectacular successes, and these equally impressive failures.[10]

It was with a sense of optimism rather than schadenfreude that more than ten years later I spoke at the commemoration of the tenth anniversary of Wharton San Francisco. My talk was titled "From Webvan to Wag: Why the New Internet Retailing Works." By then I'd seen some interesting things—such as Netgrocer.com "defying" the law of gravity and acquiring customers from over eighteen thousand separate zip codes in its first three years of operation.[11] (When it started in May 1997, it had customers in a mere thirty-four zip codes.)

I'd seen Marc Lore and Vinnie Bharara found Diapers.com back in 2005, and then add a host of other sites to it under the umbrella com-

---

10 We'll talk more about this later, but for those who are interested, here is a nice look at "10 Big Dot.Com Flops" from CNN Money: http://money.cnn.com/galleries/2010/technology/ 1003/gallery.dot_com_busts/index.html. Suffice to say that Pets.com, Webvan.com, and Kozmo.com all made the cut, entering at first, second, and ninth, respectively, on this rather ignominious list!

11 What's cool about this company (and many others) is that while it does in a sense defy gravity by acquiring customers from everywhere, a deeper understanding of what local gravity means almost perfectly explains its sales patterns.

pany Quidsi.com, from Soap.com (household supplies) to Yoyo.com (toys). In 2011, they sold the business to Amazon for $545 million.[12]

In October 2007, two graduates of the Stanford Graduate School of Business, Andy Dunn and Brian Spaly, launched Bonobos.com, the first online fashion brand to exclusively target men. Bonobos operated almost entirely in the virtual world at first, but it has since become much more active in the real one through a partnership with the retailer Nordstrom and its own Guideshops. Andy and Brian had the vision to take a "touch and feel" product (clothes) to a medium that seemed, on the surface at least, ill suited to it (pardon the pun).

In February 2010, while in their final semester of classes, Wharton School graduates Neil Blumenthal, Dave Gilboa, Andy Hunt, and Jeff Raider kicked off WarbyParker.com. They targeted a category, eyewear, that they believed was "broken" in the sense that there is a great disparity between what consumers pay for products (often several hundred dollars), and what those products actually cost to produce (perhaps twenty-five dollars). Back then (and even now) a pair of glasses produced for say $25 and labeled with a fancy brand name cost more than an iPhone.

When the team started, they estimated the annual worldwide addressable eyewear market as about $65 billion, and also noted that no more than 1 to 2 percent of the $22 billion US market was conducted online. To the founders, this seemed to be a tremendous opportunity, rather than an indication that hardly anyone wanted to buy their glasses online. Since then, Warby Parker has opened stores and showrooms, including flagship stores in Manhattan, and has sold over 500,000 pairs of glasses, most of them through WarbyParker.com. I'll return to this exciting story in the epilogue to illustrate the key ideas in this book.

In short, I've spent the past decade at the Wharton School trying to understand how these and countless other virtual-world companies get off the ground, and why some succeed and some don't. In the process,

---

12 If you'd like to listen to a wonderful interview by Jessica Harris with Marc and Vinnie on the NPR show *From Scratch* and hear more about their friendship and business, go to www .npr.org/2013/09/18/223785364/marc-lore-and-vinnie-bharara-founders-of-diapers-com. It's a great human story of family and friendship, as well as a great business story.

I've figured out that a lot of the answers rest on where customers reside and what they do in the real world.

Of course, this is not the *only* reason that some e-commerce businesses succeed and others do not. It is, however, an essential piece of the puzzle, precisely because the real world and the options available there help to define and constrain the attractiveness of specific offerings in the virtual world.

In many ways, some things seem to have come full circle since I first started studying and working with Internet companies. On June 16, 2013, Reuters covered Amazon's foray into groceries and reported that "Webvan may have been the single most expensive flame-out of the dot-com era, blowing through more than $800 million in venture capital and IPO proceeds in just over three years before shutting its doors in 2001."[13] Time will tell whether Amazon Fresh will succeed where others have failed.

Of course, there is a lot more to life than just grocery shopping — we eat out, date, learn, and buy all manner of things — so we'll be looking at a lot of other examples as well. But this book is less about trends and specific business models, and much more about everyday human behaviors: things like interacting with friends and colleagues, looking for information, and shopping for stuff offline and online — and how they are affected by where we've chosen to live in the real world.

What This Book Offers *You*, the Reader

This book is really for anyone who is curious about how and why we use the virtual world of the Internet and its related technologies to shop, sell, and search. And, more than that, it's for anyone interested in understanding how our motivations and patterns for using the Internet are rooted in our physical locations and circumstances — and how those patterns may evolve.

This group of readers includes start-up founders, managers in the

---

13 Alistair Barr, "From the Ashes of Webvan, Amazon Builds a Grocery Business," Reuters, June 16, 2013, http://in.reuters.com/article/2013/06/16/amazon-webvan-idINDEE95F04H20130616.

e-commerce sector, current and future entrepreneurs, business and economics students, professional investors, and others, such as policy makers and regulators. So, if you want a framework to bolster your knowledge of how the virtual world works, and how to succeed in it, this book is for you.

With my friends and coauthors, I've conducted much of the core research for this book myself, seeking answers to the following:

- Why do sales patterns for Internet businesses often evolve in clusters?
- Why do locations that are far apart sometimes respond in the same way to new Internet businesses, and why does "similarity" of location go way beyond geographic closeness?
- Why do people who are "different" from their neighbors, in terms of their tastes and preferences, find the virtual world especially attractive?
- Why do trust and information sharing in local offline communities help Internet businesses grow?
- Why does location matter for information to be considered credible, and who accesses that information and relies on it?

In order to answer these questions, we've analyzed data from tens of thousands of US zip codes and examined millions of transactions from consumers all over the country. We've also thought a lot about theories that explain how and why one location differs from another. On top of that, we spent countless hours running statistical models on our computers. I've also learned a tremendous amount from the work of many colleagues, writers, and commentators with whom I have not worked directly. I draw heavily on all of these sources in this book.

The use of academic research as the foundation for the book provides at least two key benefits. First, academic articles can be hard to read and access—and in this book, I do the translation work for you. The phrase "it's only academic" exists for a reason, as some academic writing can be dry and, dare I say it, a bit obvious as well. Thankfully, there is also a lot of really insightful and creative work going on in the academic world and I was able to pick out the "good bits" for this book.

Second, the studies underlying an academic article are rigorously conducted, and the final article has passed through peer review. This means that the insights we build together will be based upon robust foundations. An example of a fantastic, research-based book is *Mindless Eating*, written by my friend Brian Wansink. In describing how context shapes behavior, Brian does a great job of drawing out the key ideas from his academic work and making them accessible, fun, and interesting.

I've tried to write this book in much the same way.

Recently, I developed a new course at the Wharton School called "Digital Marketing and Electronic Commerce," and many of the ideas in this book were shaped and tested there. It goes without saying that my students in those sessions were an invaluable source of inspiration and enthusiasm for this book. While I greatly enjoyed doing the research required to prepare the course, I was frustrated by the lack of a single and unified resource on what I consider to be a defining element of the Internet: that its use and innovations are largely and systematically driven by real-world factors.

When students asked me questions, I had to refer them either to purely academic papers (not always the favorite reading material of MBAs, or undergraduates either, for that matter) or to stories and anecdotes in the business and popular press. While these latter sources are insightful and often entertaining, they are best understood when viewed through the lens of an integrative framework in a research-based book.

That's what the next two hundred or so pages are about—integrating and understanding what is currently known through principles that are more enduring. By the time you've completed this book, you'll have a firm grasp of the six key elements of real-world/virtual-world interaction. And you'll possess a structured approach, the GRAVITY framework, for understanding how virtual-world businesses become successful in particular physical locations, as well as a handy formula for testing your own ideas.

And who knows? You might even create the next Diapers.com![14]

---

14 If you're thinking of pursuing the same model in a different country, that's not a bad idea either. In fact, the Wharton graduate Davis Smith and his cousin and HBS graduate Kimball Thomas did just that, founding Baby.com.br.

GRAVITY: How the Real World Influences
the Virtual One

While this book's six chapters are self-contained, the concepts presented in each build on one another quite a bit, and for that reason the chapters in this book are probably best read in order.

In fact, there is a strong underlying logic to the layout of this book. The first two chapters set the foundation. The next three elaborate on key nuances of how the real world influences the virtual one, and the final chapter looks to the future and ties everything together.

In GEOGRAPHY I look at the key principles that explain how we decide where to live and what influences the kinds of goods and services that are available in our locations. Once we know how the real world is organized and varies from one location to another, we have a platform for understanding how the virtual world is used.

RESISTANCE shows how the real world and the virtual world interact with each other—in the consumption of both products and services as well as information and content. The real world often places obstacles in the way of our getting what we want, and the virtual world often helps us remove them.

ADJACENCY explains why it matters who is next to whom. Specifically, this chapter examines how demand patterns for virtual-world sellers spread systematically from one real-world location to the next.

VICINITY demonstrates that there is more to how things cluster in the virtual world than is explained by adjacency alone. When groups are formed in the virtual world, whether around the consumption of content or products, they are often made up of people who live far apart. The twist, however, is that these people who live far apart do share common real-world circumstances and preferences. This, in turn, drives similarities in their behavior.

ISOLATION explains the importance of the relationship we have with the people who live near us in the real world and how that affects what we do in the virtual world. On average (like it or not!), we are quite similar to our neighbors in many regards, but in situations in which we have different tastes for products and information, the virtual world liberates us in special ways.

TOPOGRAPHY concludes the book and looks to the future by explaining how products, information, and people move through and traverse the landscape of both the real and virtual worlds. I consider what happens, for example, when the virtual world goes mobile, and how the variation of real-world landscapes predicts the behavior of buyers and sellers in the virtual world.

YOU is the Epilogue. This postscript illustrates the GRAVITY framework at work, through a short case study on WarbyParker.com. It provides the key principles for how you might build a champion business or brand (including your own) in the virtual world, by leveraging your knowledge of how it's shaped by the real one.

I developed the GRAVITY framework to give you a cohesive and powerful way to understand real-world/virtual-world interaction. The idea of "commercial gravitation" is so central to how searching, shopping, and selling decisions come about that it is uniquely suited to serve as the organizing theme.

CHAPTER 1: GEOGRAPHY

How the Real World Organizes: Individual Decisions, Neighborhood Composition, and Country-Level Patterns

Chapter 1 is the foundation for this book. We can't understand how people use the virtual world unless we internalize some key ideas about GEOGRAPHY. These ideas tell us that the physical world is organized according to some simple and surprisingly robust principles.

First, I show how the choice of where we live (which city and which neighborhood) impacts the relationship that we have with the Internet. In the same way that we all have preferences for different environments—beaches versus mountains, towns and suburbs versus dense urban environments, and so on—how much we like a location as a place to live also depends on the kinds of goods and services that are offered there. This means that where we live dictates, to a great extent, how much we "need" the Internet, and for what kinds of things in particular.

I kick off chapter 1 by explaining one of my favorite research findings: the location in which we live causes us to favor one brand (e.g., Folgers coffee) over that brand's closest competitor (e.g., Maxwell House), and if we move locations, we gradually adjust our preferences to whatever the majority in the new place prefers. Next, I examine how neighborhoods are formed, who decides to live together, and what this might mean for searching, shopping, and selling online. I briefly discuss Zipf's law and central place theory, two clever ideas that show us how our offline world organizes itself. With this foundation in place, we will have a nice starting point for relating our physical geography to our online behavior. The remaining five chapters explore what this implies for our virtual-world decisions (i.e., how we shop, sell, and search online).

CHAPTER 2: RESISTANCE

Why Frictions Exist and How to Overcome Them

Chapter 2 establishes the central idea of RESISTANCE. If you've ever needed a beer on a hot day or a new TV to watch the Rugby World Cup Final or the Super Bowl, you've probably experienced the two main impediments that the real world throws in the way of our getting what we want — *search frictions* and *geographic frictions*.

Specifically, we can find it costly and irritating to search for better products and services, better prices, and so on. More fundamentally, our choice of where to live makes us captive to whatever real-world options that location throws our way. In chapter 2, I explore how local constraints and conditions influence activity that takes place in the real world, and how the Internet helps us overcome these two restrictions.

The size and demographics of a city have a major influence on whether the Internet is used mainly by those who live there as a tool for searching or as a tool for shopping. In chapter 2, I explain why, all else being equal, residents of locations that are smaller, more remote, and more homogenous are more likely to use the Internet for shopping than residents of larger locations are. In locations that are larger, more urban, and more diverse, residents are more apt to use the Internet as a source of information than residents of smaller locations would be.

Even though everything in the virtual world is just a click away in theory, in practice our real-world location constrains where we go in the virtual one. In chapter 2, I explain why rugby lovers in Philadelphia are more likely to read rugby blogs from South Africa than they are those from Australia, and why most American consumers of pornography get it from Canada and not from England.

CHAPTER 3: ADJACENCY

Why Proximity Matters: Individual Interaction, Mechanics of Adjacency, and Neighborhood Effects

In chapter 3, I describe the kinds of patterns that emerge when new Internet businesses get going, why they take the forms that they do, and why the most common and important pattern is fueled by ADJACENCY as a business evolves. This is because before we try new products we often talk to friends and acquaintances who share locations with us. In addition, we often just copy and emulate other people in our local neighborhoods. We adopt whatever they are doing after observing their behavior directly. In chapter 3, I explain why these two powerful habits—learning from others directly and copying them—underlie geographic contagion—that is, given the geography of a location and the reality of local options, there are good reasons why sales move systematically from one neighborhood to the next.

Of course, within a country or even a state, cities and neighborhoods can be quite different from each another. However, most people live in locations that contain neighbors who are similar to them in key ways. Birds of a feather do indeed flock together (something we academics call "homophily"), and this flocking has profound effects on virtual-world behavior.

Communication, emulation, and the co-location of similar kinds of people, help generate specific and predictable patterns of searching, shopping, and selling online. Whether you acknowledge it or not, you're actually quite similar to your neighbor in ways that really matter for predicting your behavior. The upshot is that customers do not simply find out about Internet sellers at random. Rather, Internet sellers will see new customers emerge from real-world locations that are adjacent to other locations that already contain similar customers.

CHAPTER 4: VICINITY

Ties That Bind: Physical Distance, Social Distance, and the Spatial Long Tail

Here I build on our discussion in chapter 3 by introducing a richer notion of "similarity" between locations. This chapter shows the many ways locations can be related, beyond just their proximate or geographic relationship and why the meaning of "vicinity" changes over the life of an Internet business. Early on, new customers are generated through "local hot spots" and tend to be clustered geographically. Over time, the pattern of customer acquisition stops being driven mainly by *proximity*. The firm starts to acquire customers in more distant — but similar — locations in terms of demographics and tastes. For example, I demonstrate how sales for a new Internet business initially took hold among a few customers in Philadelphia and Pittsburgh, and later spread to more distant locations within the state of Pennsylvania — but these distant locations were quite similar in some important ways.

For example, although Philadelphia is closer to Harrisburg (about seventy miles away) than it is to Pittsburgh (about three hundred miles away), a large fraction of the individuals who live in Philadelphia are more likely to have tastes and traits in common with their counterparts in Pittsburgh than with those living in Harrisburg.

I also explain how Internet firms should "seed" markets to best capitalize on the effects of proximity and similarity. To conclude the chapter, I illuminate something I call the Spatial Long Tail (SLT).[15] In the SLT, initial sales arise from *proximity* among close neighborhoods in

---

15 If you've read Chris Anderson's excellent book *The Long Tail: Why the Future of Business Is Selling Less of More*, you're familiar with the idea of a "Long Tail" based on the sales ranks of products. While products in the "head" sell the most units, products in the "tail," which have small sales individually, contribute a lot to the company's overall profitability when they are all added together. I give a more complete explanation of this in chapter 4 and show that a parallel idea extends to sales ranks by geographies.

large markets or "hot spots," and later sales arise from *similarity* among distant but comparable smaller neighborhoods.

This concept shows that demand often comes first from customers who are adjacent to each other, and then through customers who are similar to each other, but live increasingly farther apart.

CHAPTER 5: ISOLATION

Why Isolation Offline Means Liberation Online: How the Virtual World Empowers "Preference Minorities"

Now, of course we can't be like our neighbors in each and every regard. I like lamb shank, but some of my neighbors are vegetarian. I like to work out at home using my friend Mike Karpenko's TapoutXT routine,[16] but my neighbor Paul prefers the gym. We all have unique tastes, styles, preferences, and needs. So some of our choices inevitably fall far outside the majority in our locations. When they do, *preference isolation* results. Preference isolation is an extreme form of geographic friction. You can't get what you want locally offline because your preferences differ from the tastes of the local majority.

Almost all local sellers, including supermarkets, clothing retailers, and restaurants, cater primarily to the tastes of the local majority. If they didn't, they would go out of business. As a result, those of us who end up in the minority (in terms of preferences) have a hard time getting what we need.

For example, no matter how often and how hard I've looked, I've never found find Vegemite[17] (which is great on toast in the morning) in a Philadelphia supermarket. It could be time to stop looking (and buy it online!).

The cool takeaway here is that certain Internet sellers get disproportionately greater demand from locations where their customers are *pref-*

---

16 In addition to the great routines at www.tapoutxt.com, I really enjoy Mike's commentary. "It's a water break, not a water stoppage!" and "'To quit' does not exist!" are two favorites.

17 Vegemite is a black paste that is a by-product of the process of brewing beer. It's delicious on toast with cheese and avocado, and it is much loved by "down under" residents from Australia and New Zealand.

erence minorities. I also explain why preference isolation leads customers to be less price-sensitive, and why for a given virtual-world seller (like Diapers.com) it has a different effect for market-leading brands (like Pampers diapers) compared with niche brands (like Seventh Generation diapers).

CHAPTER 6: TOPOGRAPHY

The Evolving Landscape of the Real and Virtual Worlds: People, Goods, and Information in Play and on the Move

Chapter 6 integrates everything I discuss in chapters 1 through 5 and looks to the future. Specifically, I explain how products and information are moved around and how they end up where they need to be— in short, what characterizes the TOPOGRAPHY, or landscape, when the real and virtual worlds start to meld together.

I look at the dramatic changes in behavior that occur as we all move from a fixed to a mobile virtual world. Among other things, I show that when you take the virtual world with you, via a device such as the iPhone or Galaxy, your local environment exerts an even stronger pull on your behavior than it does when you're on a laptop.

"Social capital," or how much we like and trust each other in our local communities, has a big influence on how easy it is to learn about new things from our friends and neighbors.[18] It also plays an important role in making the transmission of information about virtual-world sellers more efficient, and it can be a big help to those sellers.

Real-world location is also a key determinant of whether word of mouth (WOM) or some other method of customer acquisition (e.g., online search) is more effective for sellers. To illustrate this point, I introduce the idea of "benefit matching" by location. That is, when you and I live next to each other in the same real-world location, a given

---

18 Broadly speaking, social capital refers to the level of trust and interaction present among members in a local community. This book uses data on social capital collected from over thirty thousand US residents by Robert Putnam of the Kennedy School at Harvard University, which are discussed in his book *Bowling Alone: The Collapse and Revival of American Community* (New York: Simon & Schuster, 2000)

virtual-world seller offers both of us an identical set of benefits, relative to our *real-world* options. So if I engage in WOM and tell you about the seller, what I'm saying will be relevant to you, and so you're more likely to act on it.

The real-world landscape impacts not only how the virtual world gets searched and delivers information, but also how physical goods are distributed. The local "topography" (e.g., tax rates, delivery times, and shopping environments) is different in each place. Continuous improvements in the information delivery and fulfillment are critical in this new landscape. Companies like Bonobos.com and WarbyParker .com that sell their own brands focus on provision of information and enhance their offerings by opening real-world locations, whereas sellers of commodities like Amazon focus on fulfillment and enhance their offerings through improved terms and delivery speed.[19]

EPILOGUE

Making GRAVITY Work For You

The epilogue shows the framework in action. To help the key ideas stick, I tell the epilogue using the inspiring story of the Warby Parker eyewear company.

You may be developing a business based on particular content or products, or you may simply be interested in furthering and enhancing your own personal brand online. Whatever you're doing, you'll be able to do it better if you understand the implications of the GRAVITY framework for charting the best way to proceed.

---

19 In a recent *60 Minutes* television interview, Jeff Bezos indicated that Amazon might use drones or "octocopters" for delivery. See Lily Hay Newman, "Amazon PrimeAir Could Deliver Your Stuff on Drones," *GizModo*, December 1, 2013.

One

GEOGRAPHY

How the Real World Organizes: Individual Decisions, Neighborhood Composition, and Country-Level Patterns

GE·OG·RA·PHY *n.*
The study of the physical features of the Earth and its atmosphere, and of human activity as it affects and is affected by these.

In the introduction I note that the first two chapters of this book, GEOGRAPHY and RESISTANCE, build our foundation for what follows. This chapter helps us understand why the real world has turned out the way that it has.

Let's get started.

Individual Decisions

CIRCUMSTANCES AND PREFERENCES

The way we use the Internet—for searching, shopping, and selling—is intimately and systematically connected to our physical circumstances.

These circumstances include the neighborhood we live in, the type of dwelling we reside in, the people we live among, and the kinds of goods and services that are served up in our local markets.

These circumstances help us determine the online products and services that appeal to various demographics and how the Internet-based businesses behind them grow both over time and across locations.

Now, of course there are other factors as well—just because my friend Lee and I live on the same floor in our apartment building doesn't mean that our behavior on the Internet is identical. Who we are in terms of demographics (age, income level, education, and socioeconomic status) and psychographics (attitude, lifestyle, and behavior) also has a large influence.

Nevertheless, for all of us, our lives in the physical world hold powerful sway over our lives in the virtual one. This chapter sets the stage for pursuing the nuances of this broad idea first by establishing a few key points about our behavior in the real world.

Throughout the book I address this real-world/virtual-world interaction and the related supporting points from three different perspectives.

First, I take into account the viewpoint of an individual decision maker. After all, understanding the "consumer" is often the starting point for insights into how to develop a successful business.

Second, I look through the lens of what goes on in a local neighborhood.

Third, I occasionally consider how the real-world/virtual-world interaction plays out in large geographic areas such as an entire country.

Individual behavior—the choices and decisions that we all make—is the foundation that generally drives everything else under study in this book, so it is typically our starting point. Additionally, our behavior in the real world happens locally in our neighborhoods; they're where we spend time with friends and family, and enjoy (or feel frustrated by) the surrounding environment, including providers of local goods and services. Many of these patterns may be extrapolated to more general patterns of behavior that can be observed across cities and even an entire country.

Thus, to get a complete perspective on how the physical world influences the virtual one, we need to view that influence through three different but related lenses: individual decisions, neighborhood composition, and country-level patterns.

Of course, our behavior as individuals is necessarily shaped by preferences (what we like) as well as by our circumstances (the conditions in which we find ourselves). Taking this line of thought a little further, we uncover a subtle interaction: our preferences for many activities, including things such as shopping and searching online, are in turn also shaped by our circumstances. A simple example about shopping online illustrates this point well.

A Diaper Story

Consider Diapers.com, the highly successful start-up founded by Marc Lore and Vinnie Bharara in 2005 and, as noted in the introduction, sold as part of a suite of sites to Amazon about five years later for $545 million.[1] Diapers.com is a dramatic illustration of how the Internet creates new markets by aggregating customers who are geographically separated yet exhibit the same basic needs.

Now, the circumstances of where and how we live in the real world impact our use of the virtual one. Taylor, a parent living in the suburbs of Houston, Texas, might have a different propensity to use Diapers .com than Paige, a parent living in downtown Philadelphia directly across from a CVS drugstore, would. This is because even if our two hypothetical customers living in these respective locations look the same (i.e., are of the same age, have the same number of children, and have comparable household incomes and lifestyles), their *offline searching and shopping costs* could still be very different.

Offline searching and shopping costs, grounded in and dictated by the real world, influence how Taylor and Paige (or anyone else for that matter) will behave in the virtual world. This is because customers in Center City, Philadelphia, and the Houston suburbs will face different prices, selections, and, of course, degrees of convenience of access to

---

1   Robin Wauters, "Confirmed: Amazon Spends $545 Million on Diapers.com Parent Quidsi," *TechCrunch*, November 8, 2010, http://techcrunch.com/2010/11/08/confirmed-amazon-spends-545-million-on-diapers-com-parent-quidsi/.

diapers and baby-related products. In fact, one immutable thing about the real world is just how much variation exists in prices and product assortments and availability from one location to the next!

I know this from firsthand experience. I've taken my measuring tape and notebook to a variety of shops in Philadelphia and actually checked prices as well as the amount of physical space reserved for different brands and products. (I'll have more to say about the somewhat embarrassing details of this real-world adventure in chapter 5, ISOLATION).

What is both interesting and important for our purposes is that Diapers .com offers *exactly the same* prices, assortment, and convenience (one-day free shipping for orders over $50) to both customers in our example. In other words, the *virtual* world is completely flat, offering the same "package" to both real-world locations.[2] But since the real-world locations for Taylor and Paige are different, the *relative attractiveness* of shopping at Diapers.com from their *given* location (Houston or Philadelphia) depends on how it compares to their offline alternatives.

Paige, the parent from Center City, Philadelphia, lives very close to an offline store. That CVS across the street is extremely easy to get to, and it's open twenty-four hours a day. The "gravitational pull" from the store to Paige is very strong. Not so for Taylor down in the suburbs of Houston. The closest offline store (with the greatest gravitational pull on her) is a couple of miles away, and the round-trip time, including parking the car and purchasing the diapers, is about thirty minutes. Not only that, but Paige in Pennsylvania does not pay taxes on diapers bought offline, whereas Taylor from Texas does. Right now, neither shopper would have to pay taxes on her *online* purchases.[3]

Putting all of this together, we see that Paige has a strong attraction

---

2 One caveat here: in the United States at least, one "nonflat" aspect of the virtual world that still pops up is the discrepancies in shipping charges that some retailers offer to different locations. These differences are evaporating in most places due to the ubiquity of free shipping and initiatives like Amazon Prime. I'll touch on this issue throughout the book.

3 Of course all this is changing. For a long time, US consumers have been able to "avoid" paying taxes on purchases made at online retailers when the online retailer is not forced to collect them. Since in many cases the online retailer has no "physical presence" in a location (the determining factor for deciding whether or not taxes have to be collected by the seller), consumers can avoid paying sales taxes. Of course, individual shoppers are supposed to remit these taxes to the government voluntarily. Needless to say, more often than not, this does not happen.

to at least one offline store, and that she faces quite reasonable prices there since no taxes are added to the regular price. In short, she has relatively low or modest "offline shopping costs."[4]

Taylor, on the other hand, has a much weaker attraction to offline stores to begin with and faces lousier prices (especially when offline taxes are figured in). She has relatively high offline shopping costs and as a result is more likely to shop at Diapers.com than Paige is.

When these individual choices are amplified throughout a neighborhood, we can start to see differences emerge across locations and, eventually, a systematic pattern of diffusion throughout individual states and the entire country.

THE FORCE OF LOCATION ON OFFLINE BEHAVIOR

Even before the Internet came along, our locations exerted a lot of influence over our behavior, whether we were fully aware of it or not. I'm not simply talking about preferences for individual products (it's rather obvious that people in Boston are more interested in snowblowers than people in Los Angeles are). There's also a lot of evidence that our preferences for individual *brands* are shaped by where we live.

I know this seems a bit hard to swallow, so let's dig into the research.

To get started, let's first explore some interesting facts about geographic variation in real-world sales patterns for *undifferentiated* products. The word "undifferentiated" is important. By this I mean products that are more or less identical and indistinguishable from each other in blind taste tests or similar comparisons (e.g., visual, olfactory, and so on).

To begin our exploration, let's go back to way before the Internet was even around. We are going to see some quite surprising things that will form the background for our understanding of the power of real-world circumstances on what we do and what we like.

We might expect to find regional differences for *differentiated* products—e.g., people in Texas like their sauces hot whereas people in

---

4   For the interested reader, a more detailed treatment of "costs of shopping" is given in Christopher Tang, David R. Bell, and Teck-Hua Ho, "Store Choice and Shopping Behavior: How Price Format Works," *California Management Review* 43, no. 2 (Winter 2001), 56–74.

California prefer them to be somewhat mild—but what we are focused on here is stuff that's identical, where no one can tell the difference.

If brands A and B can't really be distinguished from each other, then it's hard to imagine why brand A might have (say) twice the market share of brand B in a particular local market. Before you suggest that it's because brand A spends twice as much on advertising—which is a reasonable explanation—please read a little bit further.

Assume that both brands spend about the same amount on marketing. Then try to imagine why consumers in Los Angeles prefer brand A by a factor of 2:1, while consumers in Philadelphia prefer brand B by a factor of 2:1. The answer to this question about undifferentiated products illustrates the important way geography shapes our tastes.

Budweiser Beer in St. Louis, Folgers Coffee in San Francisco

What follows may seem a little counterintuitive at first—in fact, the basic finding is downright remarkable! Here's the key takeaway: our preferences for *brands themselves* are often shaped by the physical circumstances of where we live. For example, try to imagine: (a) that you drink a lot of soda (let's leave aside medical advice that suggests that you should not), and (b) that you live in Atlanta. Which of the two major brands of soda—Coke or Pepsi—are you more prone to consume? If you guessed Coke, then give yourself a pat on the back. Now repeat the same exercise for beer (Budweiser vs. Coors) and imagine that you live in St. Louis. If you guessed that you're a Budweiser drinker, take another pat and read on for the reasons why.

The answer can be found in some fascinating studies by researchers from the US and the Netherlands who shed light on the remarkable power of location and circumstance to shape sales patterns for even very basic products.[5] It turns out that relative market shares for the leading brands of widely purchased and consumed supermarket products, such

---

5   See Bart Bronnenberg, Sanjay Dhar, and J. P. Dube, "Brand History, Geography, and the Persistence of Brand Shares," *Journal of Political Economy* 117, no. 1 (February 2009), 87–115; Bart Bronnenberg, J. P. Dube, and Matt Gentzkow, "The Evolution of Brand Preferences: Evidence from Consumer Migration," *American Economic Review* 102, no. 6 (October 2012), 2472–2508.

as beer, coffee, mayonnaise, and soft drinks, vary considerably through-out the United States. This fact alone is quite surprising. After all, why should Folgers and Maxwell House coffee brands have very different market shares in different parts of the country?[6] The simple fact is that the pattern of differences systematically connects to which brand got into which market first.

Folgers's market share is much higher in San Francisco because this is where the brand was introduced way back in 1872. Similarly, Maxwell House does much better in the Northeast (the brand was launched in Nashville in 1892), where the Folgers market share is the smallest.[7]

Furthermore, this finding is incredibly robust—leading brands in numerous product categories have the largest market share in markets where they were first introduced—even though in many cases these brands were introduced over one hundred years ago. So sometimes just being first in a particular market allows you to dominate that market for decades and decades, even as new entrants come along.

Now *that* is a powerful location effect!

Academics and consultants refer to this persistence of brand loyalty as a *first-mover advantage*. This means that brands that enter a market first have the opportunity to shape consumers' preferences and also to build up better relationships with distributors than their eventual competitors.

Of direct interest to us is that first mover advantages can have a very strong geographic component. This creates a virtuous cycle for the brands in question—they enter first and have an initially higher market share, which in turn leads to better local support in their distribution channels, which further increases their market share.

---

6 I don't deny that there are die-hard brand loyalists out there who really do feel, for example, that "the best part of waking up is Folgers in your cup." But let's face it—there really is very little difference between these two options. Even consumers who express a strong preference would be unable to discern which is which in a blind taste test. In that sense, I'm willing to bet cold hard cash that coffee drinkers are no different from drinkers of soda or beer—the consumers most often subjected to blind taste tests. Note that smelling the aroma of each doesn't help either. For details, see the classic article by Ralph I. Allison and Kenneth P. Uhl, "Influence of Beer Brand Identification on Taste Perception," *Journal of Marketing Research* 1, no. 3 (August 1964), 36–39.

7 The authors of the study note on page 99, "In general, Folgers clearly dominates the ground coffee industry in the West and North Central markets. But Maxwell House dominates the East Coast."

The skeptics among you may be thinking, "I can see why that works for bigger and more involved decisions like my choice of mobile phone or airline, but it seems odd that it would work this way for basic goods bought in a grocery store." And that's a good point—phones and airline tickets are expensive, and the choices themselves create "switching costs." Once you have an iPhone and start using a lot of apps, it's harder to abandon the platform and go with a Galaxy. Similarly, the longer you're with an airline, the more points and status you accrue. This makes it hard to give all that up and go with someone else. If you fly a lot you may have found yourself stuck with a carrier that you don't really care for, just because of the access to rewards that you've earned.

If the iPhone entered a particular location before a competitor did, it would not be that surprising to see it build up a big advantage there—at least until a vastly superior alternative emerged. But for the very basic products we're discussing here, location-based differences come about from the way in which they enter markets and then generate persistence in local customers' buying habits.

That's why you're more likely to drink Coke (and not Pepsi) if you live in Atlanta and Budweiser (and not Coors) if you live in St. Louis.

Again, consider the subtle nature of this finding. It's not that somehow all of the people who like Coke decided to *live* in Atlanta and that Budweiser drinkers flocked to St. Louis. The choices made by these customers are not shaped by inherent preferences; rather, their preferences have simply been shaped by where they live.

Move, and You'll Change Coffees!

Now, please don't try to protest that you're a lifelong fan of Budweiser, you definitely prefer it to Coors, and you would know the difference in an instant. All the research based on blind taste tests indicates that you would have no shot at all. When drinkers are given beer and soda in paper cups, with the brand hidden, no one can tell what is what.[8]

---

8   You could run the test yourself or just read articles like this one, by the branding company Stealing Share: "It's Not the Taste, Stupid," www.stealingshare.com/pages/Beer:%20Its%20 Not%20The%20Taste,%20Stupid.htm.

Even drinkers who claim to have very strong preferences for one brand over another literally can't tell the difference between them.

So far we've seen that our preferences for various commodities (e.g., coffee and beer) are dictated by our physical locations. If this really is true, then we may be able to identify the effect as an undoubtedly causal one. A study in the *American Economic Review* does exactly this and clearly shows the effect of location on preferences by studying the behavior of consumers who grow up in one part of the United States and, later in life, move somewhere else.[9]

To continue with our coffee example, imagine that you grew up in Boston but later moved to San Francisco. The data show that when you move from a "Maxwell House–dominant" market (Boston) to a "Folgers-dominant" market (San Francisco), your preferences adjust to those of your new market. Most of the adjustment (about 60 percent) happens almost immediately, but the remaining adjustment takes a very long time, as I'll explain in a moment.

To see how the calculation works and how the adjustment happens, imagine that Folgers's market share is 20 percent in Boston (so that, on average, a typical consumer buys Folgers about one-fifth of the time) and 50 percent in San Francisco (so that, on average, a typical consumer buys Folgers about one-half of the time).

An individual who leaves Boston and takes up residence in San Francisco allocates about 38 percent of their coffee expenditures to Folgers almost immediately after migrating.[10] This is of course much more than the typical Bostonian (20 percent) but still less than the native San Franciscan (50 percent). According to the researchers who conducted the study, the remaining 12 percent gap (50 percent minus 38 percent) closes very slowly indeed. It will take about twenty years before half of that remaining gap, another 6 percent, is closed.

So what does this all mean? Well, our location shapes what we want,

---

9 Bart J. Bronnenberg, Jean-Pierre Dube, and Matthew Gentzkow, "The Evolution of Brand Preferences: Evidence from Consumer Migration," *American Economic Review* 102, no. 6 (October 2012), 2472–2508.

10 Note that the "market share gap" is 30 percent (50 percent in the new location minus 20 percent in the old location). Sixty percent (i.e., 60% × 30% = 18%) closes "immediately," meaning that a customer who just moved from Boston and was used to allocating roughly 20 percent of his or her coffee expenditures to Folgers will now allocate about 38% of his or her coffee expenditures to that brand. This calculation is based on statistical regression analysis from the article in *American Economic Review* cited earlier.

and because of that we adjust very quickly to our new surroundings, but only *partially*. The "location of the past" stays with us, exerting influence over us, for quite a long time!

Back to Diapers

Let's take what we've learned, return to the diapers category, and make one additional point. Given what we know now about coffee and beer, we may find it reasonable to expect that a young mother who grew up in Cincinnati (home of Procter & Gamble and the location in which Pampers diapers were first introduced), would, on average, be more apt to buy Pampers than a competing brand (such as Huggies by Kimberly-Clark, a firm founded in 1872 in Neenah, Wisconsin).

On top of this, consider that this mother lives in a neighborhood where *other* mothers typically buy Pampers diapers and frequently interact. Since the impact of geography on preferences holds for everyday products, like coffee, that are sold in supermarkets, and mostly consumed in private, it should be stronger for "socially observable" products. For example, the brands of eyewear and clothing worn by my friends and neighbors, or even the cars I see on the street, may prompt me to buy them too, or at least to chat about them.

Twin Prongs of Geography

So we have two strong, robust, and perhaps surprising impacts of *circumstances* on *preferences*. The first that is where you live impacts how you use the Internet and its related technologies to buy goods and services and to connect with others. This effect works through the force of the *offline* options that you have. (Admittedly we've only scratched the surface here as to the reasons for this, but that's what the remaining chapters are for.)

When you think about it for a bit, you can no doubt recall times when you bought something online because it either wasn't available locally or was too inconvenient to access offline.

The second effect is more subtle, but nevertheless very powerful.

The preferences you develop for the *individual brands* that you end up liking, buying, and consuming are also shaped by where you live. If you grow up in a Maxwell House town (Boston), you'll tend to prefer Maxwell House to Folgers. But then after moving to a Folgers town (San Francisco), your preferences will evolve to favor Folgers.

There are multiple drivers of this effect. For instance, Folgers is likely to be more prominent, popular, aggressively priced, and widely available in your new hometown.

A great insight from effect number two is that it operates on products that are essentially undifferentiated. By that, I mean that no matter how much you claim to love certain brands of beer, soda, coffee, and the like, there's a lot of evidence that your preferences are just an artifact of where you grew up.

On the one hand, this seems a bit depressing. You just like what you're exposed to. Yet in other product categories the effect is a lot easier to swallow. It's quite natural to imagine that products more rooted in culture, like TV comedies, for example, draw a lot of their flavor and meaning from location.

If you grow up in Manchester, England, then *The Office* means Ricky Gervais. Those from Manchester, New Hampshire, probably prefer Steve Carell. So the force of location works on all classes of products, from those in which we expect to find it, like culturally determined products, to those in which we wouldn't expect to find it at all—like undifferentiated products.

Sales of products that fall in the middle—like higher-end consumables (clothes, shoes, and so on) and durables such as consumer electronics—depend on geography as well, both through "social observability" and the willingness of neighbors to chat and share information.

Neighborhood Composition

AGGLOMERATION AND CLUSTERING

Since we now know that physical circumstances help to dictate our use of the Internet and its related technologies, and that they also drive our preferences for products and brands, it's helpful to think about how we ended up in our particular physical circumstances to begin with. Why do some of us live in Philadelphia while others choose San Francisco?

There are at least three sets of factors that shape our choice of where to call home. First, there is the force of inertia and family ties. Many of us simply choose to live close to where we grew up. There are, of course, strong cultural and personal reasons for this, and the tendency for this varies from country to country.

Researchers at the Federal Reserve in Washington, DC, and at the University of Indiana note that: "it is widely believed that internal immigration rates in the United States—that is, population flows between regions, states, and cities within a country—are higher than in other countries."[11] The data bear this out, as the authors confirm that mobility within the US is about twice that of mobility within Western European countries.

Second, there are economic barriers and incentives. For example, even if I'd like to live on Central Park West in Manhattan, an academic salary doesn't provide the necessary means. The effect of these economic factors is fairly obvious and naturally leads to a particular kind of clustering. Individuals who share the same neighborhood are likely to have similar levels of income or wealth, and to share characteristics that drive income and wealth.

Third, there is the old saying that "birds of a feather flock together." In the introduction, I provided the formal term for this, homophily. This just means that clustering on cultural and ethnic grounds is common. A drive through a large, diverse city such as Los Angeles reveals signs announcing "Little Tokyo," "Koreatown," "Little Armenia," and so on. Even though these neighborhoods are somewhat commercial—selling food and other items from the identified countries—they also contain residents who have ties to those countries and cultures.

Homophily is not just determined by cultural, ethnic, and demographic factors either. Preferences—of all types—can be an equally strong basis for it. For example, as a source or driver of homophily, political affiliation could be just as powerful as ethnicity. If you drive west

11 Raven Molloy, Christopher L. Smith, and Abigail Wozniak, "Internal Migration in the United States," *Journal of Economic Perspectives* 25, no. 3 (Summer 2011), 173.

from Koreatown in Los Angeles, you'll soon pass through West Hollywood, which is a city that is known for its liberal politics and artistically
inclined citizens.

Measuring and Understanding "Who and Where"

Thankfully, governments and commercial suppliers of marketing research put a lot of effort into collecting data about who lives where. So
we can easily measure numerous features of the real world, and if we do,
it will help us predict what will happen in the virtual one. The United
States Census, for example, provides considerable detail on income,
education, ethnicity, and so on, for every single zip code in the country.
Some commercial providers summarize and interpret data supplied by
the government and demographic and psychographic[12] profiling of zip
codes.[13]

A lot can be learned from the data, including who is using the virtual
world. A study by researchers at the University of Chicago found that
households with very low incomes (less than $20,000 per year) were
more than 20 percent less likely to get online than those with very high
incomes (more than $150,000 per year).[14] The same study found that
education has a pretty big impact as well. People who graduate from
college are about 15 percent more likely to be online than those who
haven't graduated from college. This phenomenon, that use of the Internet is related to socioeconomics and demographics, is often referred
to as the "digital divide."

There's also some very interesting evidence of "double jeopardy."

---

12 Psychographics capture attitudes, lifestyles, and behaviors, and therefore provide a nice
supplement to more readily observable and measurable demographics.

13 The company ESRI from Redlands, California, executes and markets a database called
"Tapestry Segmentation" that classifies US residential neighborhoods into sixty-five unique
market segments based on socioeconomic and demographic characteristics (see www
.esri.com/data/esri_data/tapestry). My favorite unique market segment is Group 09 "City
Lights," which comprises individuals who live in "principal urban centers," dwell in "older
homes reflecting the diversity of urban culture," and "practice yoga." It's certainly a segment
that I aspire to join (if they'd have me).

14 Ethan Lieber and Chad Syverson, "Online Versus Offline Competition" in *The Oxford
Handbook of the Digital Economy*, ed. Martin Peitz and Joel Waldfogel (New York: Oxford
University Press, 2011), 189–223.

Older people are less likely to get online to begin with, and when they are online, they're less likely to buy anything there.

And here's a really cute finding that ties location behavior not just to shopping and searching by consumers, but to the actions of sellers as well.

The authors checked whether there is any relationship between where online sellers set up shop (where they located their offices) and the number of people in that location who bought something online. Now, if geography were completely irrelevant for e-commerce, then there would be no relationship at all between these two things.

However, what the researchers found was very surprising.

When the number of shoppers in a market who buy things online increases by 10 percent, an additional two online shops open *in that location*. That is, there is a statistical relationship between the propensity of a location's citizens to shop online and for e-commerce sellers to base their businesses there.

So the real and virtual worlds are indeed inextricably linked.

PREFERENCES, LOCATION, AND MOBILITY

So far I've said quite a bit about who lives where and how this relates to online behavior. Now it's time to dig a little deeper. Beyond who, descriptively, lives in a location, there are other important sets of less obvious factors to consider when examining the real-world forces shaping our behavior in the virtual world.

One of the most fundamental is the set of individual preferences for the goods and services that the *locations themselves* are serving up. This sounds like a mouthful, so let's step through an example.

Imagine that I work in New York City and that I place a high value on access to movie theaters and interesting bars and restaurants. This set of preferences might lead to me live in Manhattan's Lower East Side. If, on the other hand, I have young children and value high-quality public schools and open spaces, I might relocate to Philadelphia's Main Line suburbs. Of course, I can exercise these preferences only if I have the means to live in my desired location.

This leads to a pretty nice insight. Knowing what goods and services are offered in a location helps us to infer something about the preferences of its residents.

Of course, it may well be that *what* people actually want in a location is also somehow related to *who* they are descriptively, but this need not be the case. So for now, let's keep three things separate: (1) economic factors, (2) cultural factors, and (3) preferences for local goods and services.

Sorting: Who *Lives* Where

Lots of studies have been conducted to try to figure out why people live where they do. The answer impacts everything from government policy to the health of the overall economy. Among the most influential ideas are those of Charles Tiebout, who, in 1956, published a theory of mobility that later came to be known as "Tiebout sorting."[15]

Tiebout argues that individuals move to locations that maximize their utility or happiness by considering the trade-offs between the benefits of the goods and services provided at a location (e.g., schools, churches, and restaurants) against the costs of living there (e.g., local taxes).

The argument is very economic in nature and assumes that individuals are perfectly mobile, have information about all of a location's costs and benefits and that the choices they make are fully rational. While these assumptions might seem questionable (economics is often referred to as the "dismal science" after all), the theory nevertheless makes a very important point.

Think about this for a moment: you are where you are right now (if you're at home) more likely than not as a result of a Tiebout-like thought process. One's neighborhood of residence is in most instances, and to a large degree, a choice, and one that is dictated by a prior assessment of costs and benefits, subject to certain constraints. Moreover, this choice, once made, will have a large and systematic influence on how you and I use the Internet for searching, selling, and shopping.

---

15 Charles Tiebout, "A Pure Theory of Local Expenditures," *Journal of Political Economy* 64, no. 5 (October 1956), 416–24.

A large-scale study of US cities and towns found, for example, that the Internet serves as a *substitute* for physical retail stores in neighborhoods where consumers have fewer offline options, and it serves as a *complement* for information in large urban areas where there is more of a need to understand "what's going on."[16]

I'll get to the important nuances of these issues in more detail in the next chapter, RESISTANCE.

Contributing and Being a Good Citizen

The last piece of the puzzle is an understanding of how people behave, with respect to their fellow residents, once they've decided where to live.

Once we're situated in a neighborhood, we don't just consume the local goods and services on offer, but we also potentially contribute to the local community. We greet our neighbors, hang out in local cafés, get involved in civic affairs, and so on. These ties among residents and their trust and interaction among one another are often referred to as "neighborhood social capital."[17] This is, from our perspective, just one more way physical locations can differ from each other. But it's a very important one.

Some neighborhoods have very little social capital and others have quite a lot. In Philadelphia, I know Christina, my local bartender, very well and sometimes receive gratis beer or an espresso, and my neighbor, Lee, looks after my apartment and my car when I am out of town.

The concept of neighborhood social capital is important. This is because once *one* individual in a location starts doing something, like buying sunglasses from WarbyParker.com, there's always a chance that he or she will tell another local resident about it. And, intuitively, we might expect that the information will be believed or trusted more in locations that have more social capital.

---

16 Todd Sinai and Joel Waldfogel, "Geography and the Internet: Is the Internet a Substitute or Complement for Cities?," *Journal of Urban Economics* 56, no. 1 (July 2004), 56–74.

17 This is a really rich topic in its own right. A fascinating and influential book by Robert Putnam, a Harvard University professor and former adviser to President Barack Obama, systematically documents the ebb and flow of neighborhood social capital over time and locations in the United States. See *Bowling Alone: The Collapse and Revival of American Community* (New York: Simon & Schuster, 2000); http://bowlingalone.com.

Social Capital and Owners Versus Renters

If a neighborhood has more homeowners, there may be less transiency, and this may have some beneficial effects in terms of the overall stability of the neighborhood. Christian Hilber at the London School of Economics was interested in this issue and tackled the question of whether homeowners make better citizens than renters do. If "better citizens" sounds a bit imprecise, just bear with me for a moment.

An initiative at the John F. Kennedy School at Harvard University called the Sagauro Seminar has collected data on trust and interaction in local communities.[18] One large data collection effort of this initiative is the Social Capital Community Benchmark Survey (SCCBS) in which over thirty thousand individuals and households throughout the United States were surveyed with questions such as "How much can you trust your neighbors?" and "How often did you hang out with friends in a public place in the last twelve months?"

After analyzing the answers to these questions, researchers can measure how much social capital exists in different neighborhoods. Hilber found something really intriguing when he matched the social capital measures from the SCCBS with other data from the American Housing Survey on the fraction of owners versus renters in different locations and discovered that home ownership does not per se increase neighborhood social capital.

So, if you're a renter, you're really not so bad for the neighborhood after all.

Home ownership *does* produce more social capital in locations in which the supply of housing is relatively *inelastic* but *does not* produce more social capital in locations in which the supply of housing is *elastic*. In plain English, this means that having more owners (versus renters) doesn't affect neighborhood social capital in newly developed areas with plenty of space to add more homes and more people, but it does in locations where there is very little room to build additional housing stock.[19]

---

18 For more information, see the Saguro Seminar's website, www.hks.harvard.edu/programs/saguaro/.

19 For more details, see Christian A. L. Hilber, "New Housing Supply and the Dilution of Social Capital," *Journal of Urban Economics* 67, no. 3 (May 2010), 419–37.

On top of this, when a neighborhood is already "built up," it's less likely that any newcomers will have as much of an influence over the already existing relationships between residents that facilitate social capital flows and formation than they would in newer neighborhoods. In chapter 6, TOPOGRAPHY, I share some of my own research showing that in real-world locations with high social capital, information passed among neighbors is more believable. This, in turn, can help drive sales in those locations for virtual-world sellers.

Country-Level Patterns

For a final piece of background, it makes sense for us to have some understanding of how the real world organizes itself at the country level. To keep things manageable we will think of an individual country, such as the United States, as the "market area" for a searcher, shopper, or seller. And, I'll look at patterns of behavior and agglomeration within this market area.

Have you ever wondered how your city stacks up against others in the country that you live in?

If so, read on.

How Cities (Unintentionally) Organize Themselves Within a Country

So far, we've seen how our individual decisions based on who we are and what we like come to influence where we choose to live. As a result, we've seen why neighborhoods form to be composed of individuals and households with similar characteristics and similar preferences.

The final question to ask and answer in this chapter is the following: How do neighborhoods cluster within a country? And specifically, is there any kind of systematic pattern to how neighborhoods or cities are organized within a country?

If we know how patterns of selling, searching, and shopping differ among cities (and why), and we know how cities are distributed throughout a country, we will automatically gain an understanding of how virtual-world patterns form at the national level.[20]

The idea is that if people within a society cluster physically in the *real* world, then perhaps their activities in the *virtual* world will also cluster in a way that is related to their physical clustering.

So let's take a look at the physical clustering.

Power Laws and Zipf's Law[21] for Cities

An established and frankly quite amazing empirical law starts us off, Zipf's law for cities (the law sometimes referred to less formally as the "rank-size" distribution). The rank-size distribution is illustrated in Figure 1.1 for the United States (if you're interested in the latest raw data, it's easily obtainable on the Internet — just search for "Zipf's law").

For now, just note that Figure 1.1 is a straight line and ranks cities in the United States according to their population size. In the next few paragraphs I'll explain how this chart and the numbers displayed on the x-axis and y-axis came about.

Although what follows is a bit technical, the pattern is quite remarkable and worth knowing about. To see Zipf's law at work and apply it, we need two pieces of information — the population of each city in the United States, and where the city ranks within the country on the basis of population.

In figure 1.1 New York City has 7.3 million people, and is ranked first; Los Angeles has 3.4 million people, and is ranked second, and so on. Once we have this information for, say, the top fifty cities, we need to transform the data a bit. Specifically, we take the natural logarithms of both the population numbers and the ranks themselves. The reason for this is rooted in the mathematics of natural logarithms and exponen-

---

20 For now we will restrict ourselves to thinking about a single country as the focus for our "offline world." Since I reside in the United States, and it's rather large and its characteristics are well documented, we will focus mainly on it.

21 George Kingsley Zipf (1902–1950) was a linguist who discovered in 1949 that in pretty much any given text, the second most common word appears about half as much as the most common word does, the third most common about a third as much, and so on.

Figure 1.1

City	2009 Population	Population Rank	Log of Population Rank	Log of Population
New York	7,333,253	1	0	15.808
Los Angeles	3,448,613	2	0.693	15.053
Chicago	2,731,743	3	1.099	14.820
Houston	1,702,086	4	1.386	14.347
Philadelphia	1,524,249	5	1.609	14.237
San Diego	1,151,977	6	1.792	13.957
Phoenix	1,048,949	7	1.946	13.863
Dallas	1,022,830	8	2.079	13.838
San Antonio	998,905	9	2.197	13.814
Detroit	992,038	10	2.303	13.808
Indianapolis	752,279	11	2.398	13.531
San Francisco	734,676	12	2.485	13.507
Baltimore	702,979	13	2.565	13.463
Jacksonville (FL)	665,070	14	2.639	13.408
Columbus (OH)	635,913	15	2.708	13.363
Milwaukee	617,044	16	2.773	13.333
San Jose	616,884	17	2.833	13.332
Memphis	614,289	18	2.890	13.328
El Paso	579,307	19	2.944	13.270
Washington, DC	567,094	20	2.996	13.248
Boston	547,725	21	3.045	13.214
Seattle	520,947	22	3.091	13.163
Austin	514,013	23	3.135	13.150
Nashville-Davidson	504,505	24	3.178	13.131
Denver	493,559	25	3.219	13.109
Cleveland	492,901	26	3.258	13.108

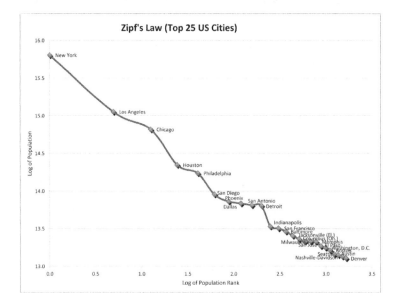

tial functions, which is in itself a fascinating and worthwhile topic (but sadly outside the scope of this book).

The intuition needed to understand Zipf's law is based on the fact that the natural log of a number can be used to tell us something about the *amount of time* needed to *achieve growth* in a quantity of interest. The quantity of interest could be money, people (or population size), the number of bacteria in a dish, and so on. To make the example straightforward, we will assume continuous compounding at 100 percent.[22]

Let's start with the simplest case.

Imagine that you have $1,000 in your savings account. How long would it take you to get "1 times $1,000" in your account, assuming a continuously compounding interest rate of 100 percent?

This may seem like a trick question, but it's actually not.

Of course, "$1,000" and "1 times $1,000" are exactly the same thing. It's not surprising then that the "natural logarithm of 1" is equal to zero. That is, it takes absolutely no time at all for your $1,000 to "grow by a factor of 1" (or, in other words, to *not* grow).

How long would it take for you to double your savings (again, assuming a rather generous 100 percent compounding rate of interest)? Well, it would take $ln[2]$ time, which is .693 (years), or about 36 weeks of a calendar year. It's going to take a bit longer to triple it; specifically, $ln[3]$ time, which is 1.098 (years), or about 57 weeks.

This same thinking applies directly to the populations of cities. All we are going to do is replace "dollars" in the example above with "numbers of people," and reverse the process a little bit.

Zipf's Law in Practice: US Cities

To see Zipf's law in action, let's use real data from actual US cities.

The natural logarithm of the population of New York City, the largest city in the United States, is $ln[7.3m] = 15.8$. The natural logarithms of the populations of Los Angeles, the second largest city in the United States,

---

22 There's a technical reason for assuming 100 percent compounding that just makes it easier to work through the example. No need to worry about the precise reasons why!

and Chicago, the third largest city in the country, are $ln[3.4m] = 15.1$, and $ln[2.7m] = 14.8$, respectively.

Above, we noted that $ln[1]$ is 0, $ln[2]$ is 0.693, and $ln[3]$ is 1.098.

If Los Angeles were expanding at a continuously compounding rate of 100 percent, it would take only 0.693 years, or 37 weeks, for it to double in size and reach around 7 million residents.

If Chicago were expanding at a continuously compounding rate of 100 percent, it would take 1.098 years, or 57 weeks, for it to triple in size and reach around 7 million residents.

Did you notice a pattern there? (Hint: Under the continuous compounding growth, Los Angeles and Chicago *both* ended up getting roughly as big as New York.)

Specifically, the *doubling* of the *second* largest city and *tripling* of the *third* largest city brings both to a number that is close to the population of the *largest* city. Of course, the time required for a lower-ranked city to reach the size of the largest city keeps getting longer as the ranks go up (i.e., while it takes Los Angeles about two-thirds of a year, it takes Chicago just over a year to reach the size of New York).

So while populations of cities decline as we go from the largest to the smallest, the time required for a lower-ranked city to become as big as the largest city keeps on going up.

This is of course true by definition. And we'd expect that.

What need not be true, but actually *is* true, is the following.

We get an approximately linear pattern when we plot the logarithm of the city populations on the vertical axis (*y*-axis) against the logarithm of population ranks on the horizontal axis (*x*-axis).

Figure 1.1 shows the nice straight-line relationship for the United States. One more bit of intuition. The *x*-axis at zero corresponds to the *y*-axis population of the largest city, "zero time" to reach "1x" of its current size, and as we know by now $ln[1] = $ zero.[23]

This approximately linear relationship between the log of the ranks of the size of a city (from first, second, third, and so on) and the log of *actual* city populations is surprisingly similar for countries the world

23 For more background, see Edward L. Glaeser, "A Tale of Many Cities," *New York Times*, Economix, April 20, 2010, http://economix.blogs.nytimes.com/2010/04/20/a-tale-of-many-cities/.

over. So, the individual cities that develop and form within a country are themselves organized systematically in terms of their relative sizes!

As noted by Steven Strogatz in the *New York Times*,[24]

... the generality of Zipf's law is astonishing. Keep in mind that this pattern emerged on its own. No city planner imposed it, and no citizens conspired to make it happen. Something is enforcing this invisible law, but we're still in the dark about what that something might be.

This is quite a useful fact and one that you can have some fun with at your next social gathering.

Thank me later.

The Stuff in Your Neighborhood

Now, if cities "organize" themselves within a country according to Zipf's law, then it may also be the case that offline commercial activity that takes place in cities might exhibit some kind of systematic pattern as well.

To get some insight into that, we turn briefly to central place theory (CPT).[25] CPT argues that, in the real or offline world, consumers visit the nearest "central places" that provide the goods and services that they need, and they make these decisions so as to minimize travel distance. The idea harkens back to the principle of "retail gravity" that was formalized in the 1930s by William J. Reilly (as discussed in the introduction).

Two concepts underlie CPT. First and foremost: there is a minimum (or *threshold*) market size that must exist before a particular good or service will be supplied to a market. If there aren't enough people, then certain kinds of stores and commercial establishments will not be built.

Second, there is a maximum distance (or *range*) that consumers are prepared to travel to procure a good or service. Beyond this distance,

---

24 Steven Strogatz, "Math and the City," *New York Times*, Opinionator, May 19, 2009, http://opinionator.blogs.nytimes.com/2009/05/19/math-and-the-city/.

25 The German geographer Walter Christaller is credited with developing this theory.

the travel cost exceeds the value a consumer places on the product. By now this second point should make good sense to us. After all, gravity dictates how much "pull" an individual seller has over us.

With these principles in place, one can then make some predictions about the kinds of goods and services that are provided in a city as a function of the size of the city itself. Larger cities, for example, have more "higher-order" or specialized goods and services available than smaller cities. For example, you might compare what's available in Manhattan with what's available in Iowa City.

So, cities are organized systematically according to Zipf's law, and offline or *real-world* commercial activity is organized according to CPT. Therefore, it stands to reason that geographic variation in online or *virtual-world* activity, whether searching, shopping, or selling, will be shaped by these fundamental forces as well. I elaborate on this in the chapters ahead.

Summary

We choose where to live. Our location choice reflects not only our constraints (e.g., our housing budget), but also our preferences for the goods and services the location offers. That's the essence of Tiebout sorting. Once we've decided where to live, our choice tends to be "sticky." Most people, even those in very mobile societies (e.g., the United States), measure their tenure in cities in years or decades.

At the neighborhood level, communities form, on average, to contain like-minded people who share similar observable traits as well. Goods and services spring up in real-world locations in predictable ways, and larger cities offer more options and more specialized goods and services. Within a country, the population is usually distributed across cities and towns according to Zipf's law, with a relatively small number of larger cities and large number of smaller towns.

So, in the real world, there is order, structure, and a fair amount of stability. Because locations vary so much from one to the next, if my offline circumstances differ from yours, then it stands to reason that my online behavior will differ too, *even if* you and I are descriptively very

similar. It follows that everything we do online will be either a complement to, or a replacement for, what we do in the real world.

Chapter 1 (GEOGRAPHY) should convince you of one basic premise.
Namely, that all this offline *real-world* clustering of people and goods
and services *must* necessarily have something to say about online *virtual-world* clustering as well.

I haven't yet explained much about *how* this all happens.

The remaining chapters in the GRAVITY framework, RESISTANCE,
ADJACENCY, VICINITY, ISOLATION, and TOPOGRAPHY, explore all aspects of how this happens, concluding with what it all means for YOU.

*You can't succeed in the virtual world unless you understand where and
how your potential customers are situated in the real one.*

Two

RESISTANCE

Why Frictions Exist and
How to Overcome Them

RE·SIS·TANCE *n.*
A force that tends to oppose or retard motion.

In chapter 1, GEOGRAPHY, we saw that the real world is organized in a structured way. Individuals choose where and how to live, and these choices lead to specific neighborhood clusters. That is, neighborhoods tend to be formed by people who share demographic characteristics, lifestyles, and preferences for certain types of goods and services. Birds of a feather do indeed flock together.

More than this, people who are in close (physical) proximity to one another tend not only to consume similar products and services, but also to share information about the things that they like. My friend and neighbor Lee often tells me about new bars and restaurants in Philadelphia; colleagues at work chat about the latest gadgets.

In this chapter, I'll look at how we navigate the real world and what that means for how we enlist the virtual world to help overcome frictions and get what we want.

Real-World Frictions

THE DIFFICULTY OF SEARCH

In the real world we all face obstacles to getting what we want. Markets don't always provide us with exactly what we'd like to know to make an informed choice, or exactly the right product for our needs and desires — let alone at the right price.

These kinds of impediments are quite stubborn and persistent, and they have been around forever. We'll use some helpful jargon and refer to them as "frictions."

This term really gets to the nature of these obstacles — they don't *absolutely prevent* you from doing things, but they do make your life more difficult. You've undoubtedly encountered them, and you have perhaps even tried to overcome them (or at least thought about how to do so).

A Fraction Too Much Friction

I am going to focus mainly on the two most pervasive and common frictions, although I'll mention one or two others along the way as well.

The first is "search friction," or the inability to get the information that you and I would like to have before making a decision. We are almost always better off having more information, such as more information about the prices we might expect to pay at certain stores, about the quality of food in restaurants, and about the experiences of others with local merchants and service providers.

Not surprisingly, economists have been studying "search" for a long time now (it's one of their most popular pursuits), so we know quite a bit about it. To see how this friction works in practice, imagine that it's 1987 and you want to buy a big-screen TV so you can watch the inaugural Rugby World Cup Final in Auckland, New Zealand.[1]

---

1   For those who like trivia, the finalists in this game were France and New Zealand, and the

Since we're back in 1987, the Internet can't help you.[2]

So you visit a local store and start to gather information about the prices and qualities of different sets. The set that you like is fairly pricey but you know there is another store across town that might have a better deal. At this point, you can either buy the set in front of you or drive across town to another store to see what they have.

Of course, to get across town you'll have to burn gas and time—i.e., incur *search costs* for the *possibility* that you will get a better product or a better price on the product that you are currently considering. The other store might have higher or lower prices, or a better (or worse) selection than the current store. Beyond this, it's impossible to know exactly what will be in stock. So, if you leave the bird in hand and traipse across town to the alternate store, you just don't know what you're going to get.

When I said that studying issues concerning search was a popular pursuit for economists, I wasn't joking. A Google search using the term "economics of search" turns up just over 500 million references!

This whopping number aside, the basic finding from the core academic literature is insightful: we keep searching for additional information until the *expected costs* of searching exceed the *expected gains*.[3]

Formal Search: Looking for a TV in the Real World

Let's continue with the TV example and imagine that the following happens: You're still standing in your local store, staring at the price tag. Kickoff time is fast approaching. You figure that it will take thirty minutes to drive across town and, based on past experience, decide that although there's a small chance the price will be better, any savings will be negligible.

---

same teams met twenty-four years later in the 2011 Rugby World Cup Final—with the same result.

2   Come to think of it, big-screen TVs might not have been around either in 1987, but let's just proceed with our scenario.

3   The word "expected" is very important here. It reflects the fact that you just don't know for certain what you're going to find, should you decide to keep searching. Your expectations come from past experiences, advertising, and so on (as I illustrate next with the TV-buying example).

On balance, you decide that it's not worth the trip, so you take out your credit card and (fairly) happily spend $1,995 on your new Sony.

In this instance, the expected costs of *additional* search exceeded the benefit, so you stopped searching and started buying. Way back in the 1960s, the Nobel laureate George Joseph Stigler formalized this idea in his article "The Economics of Information."[4] Were the expected benefit of continued search higher than the cost, you would take the *additional* trip and go to a second store.

Also, it pays to keep in mind that since different people in the real world value their time and money differently, it's quite likely that someone else faced with exactly the same outcomes would have taken the extra shopping trip.

So what does this show?

The real world has an important and pervasive friction. You have to expend effort—incur *search costs*—in order to make better decisions. This could entail searching for better prices on consumer electronics or groceries, or even shopping around for a better person to date. The virtual world is a big help, so enter Milo.com, the SaveOn! app, and OKCupid.com to solve the electronics, groceries, and dating problems, respectively.

In fact, there are literally thousands of new businesses and innovations on the Internet that have arisen to help mitigate the broadly defined *problems of search*. This is actually no surprise, considering how valuable it is to consumers for such "search" problems to be solved.

Later in this book we'll look at TripAdvisor.com—a business now valued at several billion dollars. TripAdvisor.com started as a small startup business and essentially exists thanks to *you and me* providing all its content.

For free.

So, I suspect there are still hundreds (if not thousands) of possibilities for new virtual-world businesses that will eliminate some of the real-world search frictions we all encounter every day.

Perhaps you'll start one of them.

---

4 George J. Stigler, "The Economics of Information," *The Journal of Political Economy* 69, no. 3 (June 1961), pp. 213–25.

MORE FRICTION: THE TYRANNY OF GEOGRAPHY

Take a look around the town or neighborhood that you live in. When it comes to location, size matters for two reasons. First, bigger markets (e.g., New York City, Los Angeles, and Chicago) have more people, and therefore more total demand and consumption needs and selection, than do smaller places (e.g., Sioux Falls, Iowa City, and Durham).

As a result, there's just more "stuff" around in places that are bigger. For some people, that variety, or at least the value of having options available that comes with it, makes big cities attractive places to live in.

Second, there's a higher chance there will be more people nearby like *you* when you live in a bigger city. Why, reasons of ego aside, does this matter? I explore this in more detail in chapter 5, ISOLATION, but when there are more people like you, there's a better chance that you'll get the things that you want.

Here's a quick preview.

Assume that you like corn beef hash (who doesn't?). If the chef at your local café believes that there are enough people in *total* in your neighborhood who like it, he or she might put it on the menu and make it available for breakfast. (Nice as you are, she's not making it just for you!)

Designer Jeans in Iowa, and Diapers (Again)

The Internet, however, is a great enabler for people who live in smaller markets. They can be released from the "tyranny of geography" simply by finding and ordering what they need online. If you want designer jeans that aren't available in the stores in Sioux City, you can simply go to Bluefly.com and order them.

This is how the Internet solves what I'll call geographic friction number one—you can live in Sioux City (a small market) but still have access to New York City (big market) variety.

Geographic friction number two is a little more nuanced. Even people in New York City may not get quite what they want, if what they want is a bit narrowly defined and there aren't enough others like them.

When the market is too small, no profit-seeking commercial provider will actually step in and offer something.

Of course, for certain types of products and services, the government will get involved, ensuring that things exist like broadband Internet in rural areas and libraries in small towns.[5]

The Internet liberates everyone by aggregating people, independent of their location, and creating a large, addressable market. We'll explore this aggregation idea in detail in the next three chapters, but here's a window into how it works.

Think back to Diapers.com. Would Marc and Vinnie have been as successful (or even had any success at all), if they had opened diaper stores throughout the United States?

Answer: probably not.

The reason? No matter how many babies there are in a certain location, it's unlikely that there are enough people to support a business that sells just diapers. On the other hand, if there are even a few people in each zip code who'd like to buy diapers and related products online, that quickly adds up to a lot of people! In this example, the Internet has liberated those who are "different" from those around them (even if they happen to live in a big city).

So the Internet creates markets made up of "similar" people, *independent of where they actually live.*

Think about that for a moment. It's a pretty powerful idea. We have only one physical world, and it pretty much stays put (the shifting of tectonic plates aside). Now with the Internet we can create *any number* of virtual worlds. A world of people who follow and discuss rugby? Sure, Rugby365.com. A world of people who need diapers for their newborns and who would rather not shop for them offline? Enter Diapers.com.

The key, of course, is that each virtual world can be impacted in different ways by the single, and relatively constant, real world.

---

5 For more examples of situations in which the government steps in (and why), see Joel Waldfogel's excellent book *The Tyranny of the Market: Why You Can't Always Get What You Want* (Boston: Harvard University Press, 2007).

Overcoming Search and Geographic Frictions

GETTING WHAT YOU WANT

So the Internet removes, or in many settings at least substantially mitigates, the two most intransigent and enduring market frictions. With it, you can find out the price of almost anything without leaving your house, connect with almost anyone, and buy pretty much whatever you like no matter where you live — so long as someone is willing to deliver it to you.

And you can do all this from anywhere if you have your smartphone in your pocket. (In chapter 6, I'll share a lot about how these frictions change when you and I use mobile devices versus laptops and desktops.)

Buying Stuff and Going Out

There are specific ways that we *actually use* the Internet to overcome frictions as a function of where we live. We'll discuss both products and information in this regard, but let's start with products, as this is a bit more intuitive.

If you live in New York City and I live in Iowa City, then, for me, the Internet makes up for the absence of a variety in local *products*. I can source designer jeans, organic household cleaners, and almost anything else through the miracle of the Internet. In short, the Internet acts as a *substitute* for the lack of variety at local stores.

You live in New York City, so your fashion shopping gets done in SoHo and household staples (even organic ones) can be picked up at any of the numerous Duane Reade drugstores, Whole Foods stores, and the like. Sure, you can shop online too, but for you, the need to do so is not urgent, because your local market already addresses most of your needs.

Now that we've seen what happens with products, let's turn to information. There are an overwhelming number of bars, restaurants, events, and activities in New York City. Wading through them all is quite difficult, perhaps even impossible. (It certainly would not be feasible to try to eat in every single restaurant in the city.) Hence, information about what is going on and where—and what's worth checking out—is very useful to you.

As a result, those of us who live in large cities tend, on average, to be heavier consumers of local information. The Internet *complements* the existing goods and services already in abundance—providing large-city dwellers with information that enables them to navigate all of the activities in their variety-laden locations.

Now of course both New Yorkers and Iowans buy things online *and* use the Internet for information too. What matters here is the *relative* emphasis. People in locations with less product variety and selection are more apt to turn to the Internet for goods. People in locations that offer an abundance of things to do turn to the Internet for information about how to enjoy them.

Academic studies have calculated just how important and numerically significant these effects are.

Dollars Per Mile

Central place theory (CPT), as mentioned in chapter 1, formalizes the idea that bigger markets bring about more variety of goods and services than smaller markets do. And beyond that, CPT states that there are certain natural thresholds for offerings. For example, if you live in a really small town, there might only be one supermarket and one gas station. If the town grows a bit, one more of each might spring up to accommodate the increased demand.

This concept is easy to understand when we think about physical goods and services, but as I'll show in a moment, it turns out to be true for information (or "content") too.

So, how exactly does an offline deficit in goods push you to go online?

Well, all else being equal, the farther away you live or work from a particular offline seller, the less money you'll spend there. If the seller is "too far" then you won't visit it at all.

This is retail or commerical gravity at work again.

Relatedly, the farther you have to travel to reach particular offline stores, the more likely you are to shop online. For example, if Wal-Mart is too far away, you're more likely to go to Soap.com for your detergents and household cleaning supplies.

For every extra mile that you must travel to visit a physical store, the greater the chance that you buy the item you're seeking online. One study by researchers at the University of Pennsylvania found that if you move from one mile away to five miles away from the nearest store, the gap between your online and offline spending increases by about three percent.[6] This is actually a pretty big effect!

Here's one final point about the difference between small towns and large cities.

Because of Tiebout sorting, as discussed in chapter 1,[7] it's quite likely that people who've chosen to live in smaller places just have lower consumption needs to begin with. In fact, that's almost always the case.

The Tiebout explanation is quite subtle. People who live in smaller locations have chosen them for a reason. Perhaps they have less inherent need for access to wide variety of local goods and services, or perhaps they have less income, or both. Regardless, on average, and for people in small towns especially, living a greater distance from physical stores increases a person's chance of shopping online.

Sites Per Million and Traffic Patterns

Traveling long distances to buy goods is something that we'd all rather be able to avoid doing; naturally, we'd like everything to be close by. This is what retail gravity is all about. Quite surprisingly, there are also patterns to be found in how far we are willing to "travel" for information.

Consider popular "national" websites like ESPN.com and CNN.com and ask yourself: "Where do their customers come from?" In a sense

---

6   Todd Sinai and Joel Waldfogel, "Geography and the Internet: Is the Internet a Substitute or Complement for Cities?," *Journal of Urban Economics* 56, no. 1 (July 2004), 56–74.

7   In case you didn't read chapter 1 or have forgotten what you read, Tiebout sorting refers to the fact that you and I "sort" into (or choose) neighborhoods that have the right mix of costs and benefits for us; e.g., high property taxes but excellent public schools.

there is really no "distance" or "gravity" involved in visiting a virtual location like ESPN.com. It's the same number of keystrokes away whether you live in Iowa City or LA. Hence, national sites such as ESPN.com and CNN.com draw traffic numbers from physical locations that are *roughly proportional* to the sizes of the populations of those cities.

Los Angeles has about 3.8 million residents and Iowa City has about 70,000, so that means LA is around 55 times as big. Given this, we may assume that the national sites SI.com (sports) and CNN.com (news) will have approximately fifty times as much traffic from LA as they do from Iowa City.

Now, in addition to national sites, of course, there are also myriad local ones such as PhillyToDo.com and LATourist.com, as well as "narrower" sites, like NorthernLiberties.org (which addresses the goings-on in the Northern Liberties section of Philadelphia) or Weho.org (focused on West Hollywood in Los Angeles). The sheer *number* of these kinds of sites and their *traffic patterns* are also explained by their users' physical locations.

To see what happens here, let's first focus on the *number* of local sites.

Research shows that the larger the city, the *more* local sites there are that serve up content devoted to the people, places, and activities that define it. One study found that adding an additional one million residents in a US Metropolitan Statistical Area (MSA), an area that can cover more than one city, brings forth about another 50–60 sites devoted solely to content pertaining directly to it.[8]

Back in the 1930s, way before the virtual world even existed at all, CPT told us that in the real world the supply of goods and services increases along with the population. Moreover, Reilly's retail gravitation model told us that physical stores have fixed trading areas, beyond which they have no hold over customers. So it's fascinating to see, more than eighty years later, how these ideas have a similar message about the production and consumption of information in the virtual world as well.

As we've established, larger cities have a greater number of sites devoted to them, and the amount of traffic that a national site such as

---

8   Sinai and Waldfogel, "Geography and the Internet."

ESPN.com gets from a given location is roughly proportional to the population in that location. The patterns for local sites however, are quite different. (Hint: keeping thinking about our principle of gravity— the farther away you get from a particular good or service location, the less likely you are to use it.)

PhillyToDo.com generates almost all of its traffic from people residing within the greater Philadelphia area. Thus, a local site serving up information is a bit like an offline store selling goods. Retail gravity plays an important role. It's still more important for physical stores than it is for virtual sites—no one will drive from Philadelphia to buy groceries at the Ralph's supermarket in West Hollywood, but some West Hollywood residents may be inclined to "travel" to PhillyToDo.com if they're planning an upcoming trip to the City of Brotherly Love.

Buying Coffee Makers Online

Some really fascinating and counterintuitive things unfold when real worlds, virtual worlds, products, and information are all combined as part of an overall shopping option for consumers.

Let's dig into an example.

Specifically, let's consider what happens when a store offers you BOPS. Not sure that you want this painful-sounding service? Relax, it's just another retail acronym—it means "Buy Online, Pick up in Store." When a store offers BOPS, you can go online and check out, say, a new espresso maker or a duvet, buy it, and then wander by the store and pick it up from there.

Let's look at all the ways this option helps you. You can reduce your *search* friction because you know the price of the espresso machine, and you also know that it's in stock (if it wasn't in stock the store wouldn't give you the option of picking it up). On top of that, you don't have to deal with a major pain point of online shopping: waiting for that package to arrive with your new shoes, duvet, coffee machine, or what have you.

This is an important issue for shopping in the virtual world, so let's take a short detour and explore a key research finding. George Lowenstein at Carnegie Mellon University conducted a clever study with a series of three experiments to measure just how annoying waiting is.[9]

The subjects in the experiments were exposed to hypothetical purchases of VCRs (remember them), gift certificates for restaurants, and gift certificates for local record shops (remember them as well?) and told that their purchases would be delivered to them in a set time period. Subjects in a "delay" condition were asked how much they would need to be compensated for the inconvenience of an unexpected two-day delay. Other subjects were told that their shipments could actually be expedited if they so desired. They were asked how much they would be willing to pay for the delivery to be expedited.

So, one group has to *be paid* for a two-day delay and another is *asked to pay* for a two-day speed up.

In each experiment, the subjects in the "delay" group wanted more compensation than those in the "expedited" group were willing to pay, even though the amount of time involved was *exactly the same* for both groups. This phenomenon was coined the "delay premium," and means that you and I need to be *paid more* to have to wait longer than expected, compared with how much we'd be *willing to pay* to shorten the wait time by the same amount.

So in some sense, BOPS gives you the best of both worlds (full information before purchase and no waiting for delivery, although you do of course have to stop by the store to pick the thing up). As a side note, *geographic* friction doesn't really apply in this example—to the extent that the store is at least offering you a decent selection of coffee machines and other products that you're interested in.[10]

Santiago Gallino at Dartmouth College and Toni Moreno at Northwestern University dug into the effect of BOPS and analyzed the sales

9 For details, see George F. Loewenstein, "Frames of Mind in Intertemporal Choice," *Management Science* 30, no. 2 (February 1988), 200–214. Some shoppers also take note of whether the prices they see in stores are favorable, compared with what they recall from their last shopping experience. When they are favorable, consumers accelerate their purchases, and when they're unfavorable, they delay them. For details, see David R. Bell and Randolph Bucklin, "The Role of Internal Reference Points in the Category Purchase Decision," *Journal of Consumer Research* 26, no. 2 (September 1999), 128–43.

10 Throughout the book I'll continue to use the term "geographic friction" to mean that a specific location is "trapping" customers by not giving them enough variety.

data for a major US retail chain specializing in housewares and with more than eighty stores.[11] One very nice feature of the study is that the chain had stores in both the United States and Canada, and the BOPS option was offered only to shoppers in the former. Gallino and Moreno could then see what happened to sales in the two countries—one that had BOPS and one that didn't.[12]

After BOPS was made available to US consumers, Moreno and Gallino expected to find that online sales in the States would go up. US shoppers should be much more willing to buy online now that they could do so without the downside of waiting for their stuff to arrive.

Surprisingly, that didn't happen—at all.

Online sales went *down*.

Yes, that's right. Online sales went *down*, even though website traffic went *up*.

So, what happened? Well, the explanation for this paradox relates to one final "friction" that applies when certain kinds of goods are available online.

I'll give the details in a moment but a little historical segue helps here.

In 1994 Jeff Bezos founded Amazon—arguably one of the most brilliant innovations in retail. (And I'm not just saying that because Amazon is publishing this book!) At that time, not much was being sold online at all; however, there had been a rather large catalog business in the United States for the best part of the past one hundred years.

So what product category, in 1994, was the leader in catalog sales? (Clue: it wasn't books.)

It was apparel.

Why didn't Jeff Bezos start selling apparel online at Amazon right off the bat? Because he realized that apparel might not be the best fit to the new medium of the Internet.

The reason?

Most of us like to try clothes on before buying them. Clothes have

---

11 Santiago Gallino and Toni Moreno, "Integration of Online and Offline Channels in Retail: The Impact of Sharing Reliable Inventory Information," *Management Science* (forthcoming).

12 This works as a sort of "natural experiment," in the sense that one group just so happened to experience something that the other did not. As such, it's an ideal approach for teasing out how particular interventions affect behavior or other outcomes. We will see a few more examples later in this chapter.

tactile, or "touch and feel," attributes that are hard to communicate online. Jeff Bezos rightly recognized that this would be a barrier to purchase, so he went way down to the twenty-fifth most popular product category sold at the time via catalogs: books. They were a perfect fit for the Internet. There is nothing about a book that you really need to touch and feel. If you know the price, the author, what it's about, and perhaps a bit of information from reviews, then you're good to go.

Now, back to the present.

Moreno and Gallino realized that the same kind of thing was happening with BOPS, since most of the products sold by the retailer they studied—housewares, home accessories, furniture, and related items— also had touch and feel attributes.[13]

Traffic at the website was up because shoppers could go online to get price and in-stock information before buying (the Internet had reduced their search friction), but they still wanted to turn on the coffee machine, sit on the sofa, or touch the duvet before buying.

So they didn't actually *buy* what they wanted online. Having confirmed the price and that the item was in stock, they went to the store to inspect the product. Hence, sales at the *store* went up.

The nice insight here is that the virtual world removed some of the frictions (i.e., knowledge of price and in-stock position) but not all of them. The real world still had a role to play because shoppers wanted to sample the products before buying them.

Nevertheless, BOPS was a great success because it led to—wait for it—ROPO (Research Online, Purchase Offline).

---

13 Without wanting to confuse things, I should introduce a little more marketing terminology. This jargon is helpful for our discussion in this book and beyond, so please bear with me. Academics refer to three different kinds of products and product attributes: *search, experience,* and *credence.* The first term is a bit confusing, given the way we've already used "search," but here goes: A *search* good is one for which you know exactly what you are going to get, even before you buy it. Think of Dunkin' Donut's coffee. (Of course, this presumes that you've already purchased the coffee before in a real-world location.) You know how it will taste *before* you order it. There's no surprise. *Experience* goods on the other hand are those for which you don't really know what you're going to get until you start touching, feeling, or consuming them. Examples are men's suits and even MBA degrees. With *credence* goods, you often still don't know how you feel about them even *after* you've consumed them. Surgery and management consulting are examples. You paid for your surgery or consulting report, and yet you still don't know whether the surgery worked (although you might feel OK) or whether the advice was any good (although the consultants had fancy degrees and were always nicely dressed).

Amazon in the Virtual World Versus Booksellers
in the Real World

Common occurrences when shopping for everyday products also afford us a nice window into how the real and virtual worlds interact. Most of us have bought a book from Amazon, and quite a few of us have shopped for books in a Walmart or a Barnes and Noble. So, imagine that you've been buying your books from Amazon and also that there are no physical bookstores near you. Now, let's see what might happen if Barnes and Noble suddenly opens a bookstore in your neighborhood just a few blocks away. Will your access to this new store change your book-buying habits on Amazon.com?

Well, for starters, you now might immediately be able to satisfy your craving to read. You can potentially get the book you want by just going down the street to the bookstore.

Researchers in the United States and Canada discovered there was a neat twist to how this happens.[14]

Say that you want a copy of *Harry Potter and the Sorcerer's Stone* to read on your Fourth of July vacation—you might now just go directly to Barnes and Noble to get it. As a result, Amazon.com starts to lose sales on *Harry Potter* in the zip codes around the area where the new store has opened. Again, because sales at physical stores are subject to commerical gravity, Amazon.com will *not* lose sales in zip codes that are more distant from the new store, since by definition they are outside the trading area for the store.

If your reading tastes lean a little more eclectic—say you want to read *Richie McCaw: The Open Side*—then Amazon.com isn't likely to suffer. This is because you're going to think twice about trudging to the store to buy this particular book.

Why the difference?

Well, when an item is as *popular* as the Harry Potter book most certainly is, then Barnes and Noble—a store with limited space—will make sure to stock it. Thanks to this fact, you can happily wander over to Barnes and Noble, safe in the knowledge that the book will almost

---

14 Chris Forman, Anindya Ghose, and Avi Goldfarb, "Competition Between Local and Electronic Markets: How the Benefit of Buying Online Depends on Where You Live," *Management Science* 55, no. 1 (January 2009), 47–57.

surely be available and that your craving to read it right away will be met.

When the item is rarer or a niche product (as a Kiwi, I can't bring myself to deem any book about our national game, rugby, or an All Black captain as "unpopular"), you'll make a different choice. You will (rightly) suspect that it's not really in the interests of the store to carry a book that doesn't have broad appeal. You're safe to bet that the product will *not* be available offline.

It will, however, probably be accessible from Amazon in a single click.

This is why sales of popular items at Amazon.com will go down in zip codes contained in the trading of the new store after it opens, but sales of niche items will not. Beyond this, Amazon's discounts will be less effective—Amazon has to do more to get your business once a physical competitor enters your market. Once again, the characteristics of the physical world have an important sway over shopping and selling in the virtual world.[15]

Gravity and "Cross-Border" Trade in Goods and Information

The Noble laureate and popular *New York Times* columnist Paul Krugman is a pioneer in the academic field of economic geography, and his core ideas are quite relevant for our discussion. A key one is that *international trade* between countries is shaped by gravitylike principles. (Yes, gravity again!)

Specifically, trade is *less* likely when countries are far apart and when their economies are of relatively disparate sizes. Trade is *more* likely between countries that are close geographically and similar in size economically.

---

15 As you might imagine, Amazon of course carries considerably more titles to begin with. Some researchers at MIT calculated that the entry of Amazon into the book market led to significant gains for consumers in terms of access to variety. See Erik Brynjolfsson, Jeffrey Hu, and Michael Smith, "Consumer Surplus in the Digital Economy: Estimating the Value of Increased Product Variety at Online Booksellers," *Management Science* 49, no. 1 (January 2003), 1580–96.

Again, this is largely due to frictions—New Zealand and the United States not only are far away from each other but also have very different size economies (the United States has the largest economy of any country; New Zealand is much further down on that list).[16]

There are generally significant *travel frictions* between the two countries, and greater disparities in business cultures among countries of disparate sizes. Thus, a simple application of commercial gravity suggests that there should be more trade between and Australia and New Zealand and between the United States and Canada than there is between the United States and New Zealand.

VIRTUAL-WORLD GRAVITY

It's pretty obvious that trade in physical goods, which have to be moved around, would be constrained somewhat by the distance between trading partners. And this is especially true for things that are heavy, bulky, expensive, and just plain hard to move. Researchers at the University of Chicago discovered a nice parallel fact when they looked at sales being transacted online.[17] They found that goods with a high value-to-weight ratio were the most likely candidates to be sold via e-commerce.

Now let's push our intuition a bit and try to imagine whether *virtual goods* would be affected by distance in the same way.

Why Americans Get Rugby News from South Africa and Pornography from Canada

Imagine that you live in Philadelphia and are interested in hardy sports. (If you live in Philadelphia, then you certainly need to be a hardy fan, given the typical performance of our pro teams.)

---

16 I am, however, happy to report that New Zealand is, according to the *Economist*, number one on the corruption index (i.e., the least corrupt country and, of course, less corrupt than neighboring Australia is).

17 Ethan Lieber and Chad Syverson, "Online Versus Offline Competition," in *The Oxford Handbook for the Digital Economy*, ed. Martin Peitz and Joel Waldfogel (New York: Oxford University Press, 2011), 189–223.

Let's say that you are interested in rugby in particular.

RugbyHeaven.com (hosted by the *Sydney Morning Herald*) is an option for content, as is Rugby365.com, based in Cape Town. Each site is just a click away, but Australia is a bit farther from the United States than South Africa is. So, to which site will you, our intrepid rugby lover, go?

Incredibly, it turns out that *content on the Internet is subject to the laws of gravity as well,* even though there are no apparent "travel costs." (Of course, we need to control for the obvious effect of language — even if you live in San Diego, you are unlikely to visit the website of the Spanish-language *El Sol de Tijuana* if the full extent of your Spanish is *Yo no hablo español.*)

A clever study by researchers in Canada examined this issue by looking at the country of origin of over nine thousand sites visited by US consumers. The sites were hosted in thirty-seven different countries — alphabetically from Australia to Slovakia (yes, New Zealand was included too) — and covered a range of different types of content, from software to games to music.

It may not come as a revelation to know that for fourteen of the thirty-seven countries, the most popular content category visited by US citizens was pornography! In fact, it was the *only* thing from Hungary, Indonesia, and Luxembourg that this particular sample of US surfers consumed.

Surprisingly, and counter to our likely instinct that distance should have no impact on consumption of content, the authors of the study found that, on average, for every 1 percent increase in the distance between the country that you live in and some foreign place, there's a corresponding 2 percent decrease in the chance that you will visit a site hosted in that country.[18] This effect of distance holds *after controlling for* (or eliminating) the effects of language differences and demographic factors.

Now, this average effect has some interesting nuances. When consumers have to pay for the content, information, or goods, the deterring effect of distance on "travel" to a foreign website for content strengthens to 2.7 percent; when these things are free, the deterring effect weakens

---

18 Bernado Blum and Avi Goldfarb, "Does the Internet Defy the Law of Gravity?" *Journal of International Economics* 70, no. 2 (December 2006), 384–405.

and declines to 1.1 percent. But perhaps the most interesting nuance is the difference between taste-dependent categories (gambling, games, music, and pornography) and non-taste-dependent categories (encyclopedias, software and technology information, and financial content).

For non-taste-dependent categories, distance doesn't matter at all; i.e., there is no statistically significant effect of distance on consumers' behavior. US consumers are just as happy getting financial information from Australia as they are getting it from South Africa.

Not so for taste-dependent categories, where the deterring effect of distance on "travel" to foreign websites is a whopping 3.5 percent for every 1 percent further the host country is from the US. Now in the interests of taste, I'll move away from pornography (the most popular category of foreign content overall for US citizens) and instead consider "rugby chat" as a cultural or taste-dependent product category for the purposes of an example to illustrate the point that I just made.

The distance between Philadelphia and Sydney is about 9,100 miles, and the distance between Philadelphia and Cape Town is about 7,800 miles. Getting to Sydney involves about 17% more distance to travel. So, whatever chance our Philly rugby fan has of going to Rugby365 .com (hosted in Cape Town, South Africa), he is more than 50 percent *less* likely to go RugbyHeaven.com (hosted in Sydney, Australia)! This is because Sydney is about 17 percent farther "away" and each percentage point reduces the likelihood by 3.5 percent, for a total of 51.5 percent.

What makes this so interesting is that there is literally no additional cost or travel time to clicking on a South African versus an Australian site about essentially the same thing.

The theory underlying this finding is that the closer that creators and users of content are to each other in the real world, the likelier they are to have similar interests or tastes. This means that the consumers of content—people like you and me—are more comfortable getting our content from sites hosted in places that are physically closer to us. Distance is a proxy for cultural similarity.

There's actually a nice parallel here to our "Folgers in San Francisco and Budweiser in St. Louis" story from the last chapter. There we learned that location matters a lot in our choice of undifferentiated products. And here we see that it seems to matter for content that is at least somewhat generic as well. Believe me, there isn't *that* much difference between the news at Rugby Heaven (www.smh.com.au/rugby-union) or at Rugby365, the South African–based site (www.rugby365.com/).

Even though the entire virtual world is now fully accessible to anyone with an Internet-enabled device, people who live in different places are, after all, still quite different in important ways. Culture and affinity affect the ways in which you and I search the virtual world.

So, there you have it.

Location and gravity matter even though the travel cost (in this case a few clicks) is, for all practical purposes, zero.

Washing Machines, Beer, and the Price of "Mesothelioma"

We've already seen that *what* you search for online, and *how often* you search, depends quite a lot on where you live. It turns out that what sellers are willing to pay to be noticed via online ads when we do these searches depends a lot on real-world factors too.

To get some feeling for this insight, let's reflect again on the real world. Many of us (myself included) are quite used to feeling the effect of local laws on our behavior. Local liquor laws, for example, can dictate whether you can buy alcohol on a Sunday, or whether you can get a beer from the supermarket.

If, like me, you live in a city like Philadelphia that charges sales taxes on white goods, you might drive elsewhere (Wilmington, Delaware, in my case) to buy your next washing machine or refrigerator. By doing so, you can save a few hundred dollars. You feel good about the money in your pocket—and perhaps also that you thwarted the (Tax) Man.

For years people have been doing this throughout the United States (and throughout the world in places where countries and states have conveniently traversable borders) and for all sorts of products. Beer is a notable category. Shoppers in Clarksville, Indiana, often cross the Ohio River on Sunday to buy cold beer in Louisville, Kentucky.[19]

---

19 "Indiana's Peculiar Liquor Laws May Drive You to Drink," editorial, *Indiana Star*, May 18, 2013, www.indystar.com/article/20130518/OPINION08/305180019/Editorial-Indiana-s-peculiar-liquor-laws-may-drive-you-drink.

Likewise, Diapers.com gets a boost in sales from locations with high offline sales taxes. The reason? Until recently, shoppers in many states could avoid paying taxes on online purchases. As a result, people living in those states with high offline taxes made relatively more online purchases.[20]

These examples and those of our earlier discussion highlight that there are times when each of us might free ourselves from the limits of our physical locations. And while these examples have focused on physical goods, we see similar patterns for content as well. If you've driven down Interstate 95 near Philadelphia recently (post May 2013) you might have seen a billboard for (855) U-CAN-SUE, hosted by the "Philly Legal Eagles."[21]

Now, what if the Legal Eagles were unable to place their sign on I-95? (Some might say that would be a good thing.) Let's say that the state did not allow lawyers to advertise. If they were barred from advertising offline in the real world, would they have to pay more online, in the virtual world, to position their business online to reach some aggrieved, would-be plaintiffs doing Google searches?

The answer is yes, they would.

Catherine Tucker from MIT and Avi Goldfarb from the University of Toronto looked into this issue. They examined how much sellers in different states (in this case attorneys) were willing to pay to bid on certain keywords to advertise their services. It just so happens that some states don't let lawyers "chase ambulances," i.e., try to contact people who have recently experienced a painful injury or a wrongful death in their immediate family.

Tucker and Goldfarb examined the prices bid for keywords in states in which direct solicitation (through offline mail, for example) by attorneys for personal injury or wrongful death suits was prohibited.[22] Then they compared the prices in these locations with the prices that were paid in states in which offline solicitation was allowed.

---

20 Jeonghye Choi, David R. Bell and Leonard Lodish, "Traditional and IS-Enabled Customer Acquisition on the Internet," *Management Science*, 58, no. 4 (April 2012), 754–69.

21 "The Philly Legal Eagles, Rizio, Hamilton & Kane, P.C., Debuting New Billboard Location On I-95 May 13th," press release, PRWeb, May 9, 2013, http://www.prweb.com/releases/prweb2013/5/prweb10716174.htm.

22 Avi Goldfarb and Catherine Tucker, "Search Engine Advertising: Channel Substitution When Pricing Ads to Context," *Management Science* 57, no. 3 (March 2011), 458–70.

Sure enough, in states in which lawyers faced *offline* restrictions, sellers (lawyers) had to pay a lot more for terms like "car accident," "medical malpractice," and my all-time personal favorite, "mesothelioma."[23]

The overall price premium in those restricted states was perhaps 5 to 7 percent, which is really quite a lot. That is, attorneys would have to pay 5 to 7 percent more *online* for those words than they would have to pay in some *other* location where the offline billboards were allowed.

Inclement Weather, Social Networks, and WindSurfing in Switzerland

Academic creativity was running high when researchers at Columbia and Stanford Universities collaborated with a coauthor in St. Gallen, Switzerland, and became interested in understanding how a real-world phenomenon—changes in the weather—affected virtual-world activity (posting on blogs and social networks) and ultimately created value for sellers.[24]

The authors collected their data from Soulrider.com, a Swiss windsurfing and snowboarding website with over ten thousand members.[25] They found that the most blogging occurred at times and locations when there was more variation in wind speed in the real world—i.e., they found that a real-world phenomenon drove activity in the virtual one. The higher the speeds at a location, the more blogging that occurred at that location—so the geographic distributions of blogging and windspeeds were positively correlated. More than that, however, the authors found that social networks are subject to "network effects in content generation."

What does this mean, exactly?

This means that they found that this incremental blogging also led

---

23 This is often cited as one of the most expensive words one can bid on—costing up to $140 per click in some instances.

24 Scott Shriver, Harikesh Nair, and Reto Hofstetter, "Social Ties and User-Generated Content: Evidence from an Online Social Network," *Management Science* 59, no. 6 (June 2013), 1425–43.

25 As a former resident of New Zealand, a place with ample beaches that were immortalized in the movie *Endless Summer*, I find it a bit hard to come to terms with "European surfing." Nevertheless, the insights from the study are worth knowing about!

to more friend requests, which in turn generated *more* blogging. So, if a given user generated more social connections, then that user would also generate more content. This creates a virtuous cycle of content creation and reciprocation, which can in turn increase the value of a social networking site (SNS).

While owners of an SNS can't control the wind, this finding is beneficial to sellers (in this case the owner of the SNS and the various clients who may want to advertise on it) because it clearly shows that events in the real world directly precipitate ties and content in the virtual one.

Summary

The real world puts obstacles in our way. Important information (e.g., about prices and product quality) can be hard to come by or costly to obtain, and not all products and services are offered in all locations. The virtual world helps us to overcome these search and geographic frictions, often eliminating them entirely. However, the Internet sometimes imposes frictions of its own — by making us wait for delivery of things bought online, or by making us uneasy about buying products with "touch and feel" components.

So, the real and virtual worlds compete with *and* complement each other. In the virtual world, you can get all the information you need about a great espresso machine for your home — you can check the price and see that it's in stock — but you still might want to visit a real-world store and "taste the coffee" before buying. You might begin your journey searching in the virtual world, and end it by shopping in the real one.

If you live in Philadelphia, you can get all the rugby news you want from either the Cape Town– or the Sydney-based website. Even though the "travel cost" of visiting either website is zero, you strongly prefer the former site because it's produced in a country that is closer to you. Among all the findings we've reviewed in this chapter, I find this especially intriguing. Gravity still holds sway over the way we consume *content and information goods* in the virtual world!

In chapters 1 (GEOGRAPHY) and 2 (RESISTANCE) we've laid the foundation for why the real world is so important and for why and how the real and virtual worlds interact and compete to deliver goods, services, and information.

The key to overcoming resistance is to understand all the ways consumers are "frustrated by frictions." The next part of the book—section A-V-I—discusses how you and I learn about what's available virtually, how we affiliate with others online, and how we liberate ourselves from the deficiencies of our real-world locations.

Frictions frustrate in the real and virtual worlds—you'll succeed in both when you identify and eliminate them.

Three

ADJACENCY

Why Proximity Matters: Individual Interaction, Adjacency Mechanics, and Neighborhood Effects

AD•JA•CEN•CY *n.*
The state of being so near as to be touching. The state of being adjacent; contiguity.

In chapter 2, RESISTANCE, we looked at the frictions that the real world puts in the way of our getting what we want. I explained how the virtual world sometimes, but not always, helps us to overcome them. Sometimes the two worlds complement each other. For example, you go to the online site of a local store to confirm that the coffee machine you want is available (in inventory) and to see how much it costs.

Satisfied that the product is there and the deal is good, you visit the store to test it out and buy it.

Other times the virtual world acts as a superior substitute for the available real-world options. If, for example, you want a niche book like *Richie McCaw: The Open Side*, and you want it as soon as possible, you should order it from Amazon and not bother to visit that newly opened bookstore down the street. Local stores with space constraints and relatively limited trading areas are not motivated to carry slow-moving items.

So, Amazon.com makes up for your lack of local variety in rugby books.

Beyond this kind of economic interaction between the real and virtual worlds, there are important interactions between individuals that are fueled by proximity. These include the relationships between neighbors in both the real and virtual worlds and the behaviors that these associations foster. In this chapter, I look at how adjacency helps to drive what happens in both worlds and how the two of them interact. I'll start by explaining some basic principles of interaction between adjacent individuals, and then I'll present a more formal way of thinking about adjacencies for individuals, and for locations as well. I'll then go over some research that looks at so-called neighborhood effects and patterns in behavior produced by adjacency.

Adjacency and Individual Interaction

Before getting started, I need to point out an important connection between this chapter (ADJACENCY) and the next one (VICINITY). This one looks at what happens in the virtual world as a result of proximate individuals sharing *locations*. The next one looks at what happens when individuals share *characteristics* or *preferences independent of the locations that they live in*. Of course, in chapter 1 (GEOGRAPHY) we learned that the Tiebout sorting principle means that individuals who share locations can also share characteristics and preferences too. So you might notice some rather complementary material over the next two chapters. I'm leading with a discussion of adjacency because the concept forms a logical building block for the concept of vicinity.

COMMUNICATION AMONG ADJACENT INDIVIDUALS

"Where's Good for Breakfast?" and the Four Pillars of Communication

As you might imagine, social interaction is a pretty big topic in its own right, with many interesting components. I won't touch on them all, just the pieces that matter for our story. For example, it has long been known that word-of-mouth communication (one common driver of social influence) is typically much more effective than overtly commercial forms of communication like advertising.[1] For our purposes, it's enough to know a few things about how this works and the vital role that is played by adjacency.

Just being next to someone can lead to good things, as it makes it easy for information to be passed from one person to the other. It can lead to bad things too, as the information may not be positive or even truthful—more about that in a bit. The important thing to keep in mind—I'll give examples soon—is that the veracity and usefulness of information in the virtual world have a lot to do with the real-world locations of the senders and recipients.

Also, while information often flows between just two people at a time, it doesn't have to stop there. I learned about Café La Maude in Philadelphia from my friend Roland,[2] and since I enjoyed it so much I happened to recommend it to my neighbor and friend Lee.

Lee in turn, no doubt, told a few friends as well.

It's rather apt that this process, which is facilitated by adjacency, often goes by the formal term "social contagion." It's "social" because people are interacting and sharing information, or at least observing what others are doing. It's considered a form of "contagion" because the spreading of ideas, behaviors, and so on requires some form of contact.[3]

Think about information spreading among friends or neighbors who live near each other and talk often. Once you picture this, it's easier to think about how social contagion is facilitated by technology—online reviews, social media, and so on—and how it works for people who might be "adjacent" to each other in some other sense (I pick this idea up in chapter 4, VICINITY). From here, we can gain insights into how interaction takes place even among people who have never met or had

---

1 For a classic reference, see Elihu Katz and Paul Lazarsfeld, *Personal Influence* (Glencoe, IL: Free Press, 1955). For an updated study on what makes certain forms of content more likely to be shared check out Jonah Berger's excellent book, *Contagious: Why Things Catch On* (New York: Simon & Schuster, 2013).

2 I met Roland at a bar managed by Craig, who is a friend of my good friend Ziv. These sorts of social chains can be quite long (I'm sure you can think of many examples from your own experience).

3 It's a bit like the spreading of the flu or the common cold (although typically more pleasant).

a face-to-face conversation. And, most important for our purposes, we can get a sense of how the age-old spreading of information in the real world impacts what's going on in the virtual world (and vice versa to some extent).

When we look at social contagion derived from adjacency, we look at: *who*, *where*, *how*, and *what*.

Let's say the "who" are the friends and acquaintances one comes across locally; the "where" is the local neighborhood; and the "how" is either via direct communication (a person-to-person conversation) or observation. The "what" is the content. The glue that holds everything together for our analysis is the real-world location, the "where."

It's pretty easy to think of examples of social contagion on a spectacular scale that involve many complete strangers as well. The more than 600 million views of Psy's "Gangnam Style" video on YouTube that went viral in early 2012 didn't all come from the singer's family and friends in Seoul. This example also shows that contagion can occur over large distances, but for now I am going to focus on relatively short physical distances and defer our discussion of "long-distance" interaction to chapter 4 (VICINITY).[4]

As to the "what"—well, that's the information itself, and there are two things to keep in mind in relation to it, starting with the richness of the message. I didn't just say to my neighbor Lee, "Try Café La Maude!" Instead, I went into some detail about my favorite items on the menu, the best time of day to visit, and so on. We ended up having a lengthy conversation about food. Because Lee and I live in an identical real-world location (the same apartment building), and the topic of conversation (the restaurant) was local, this information was useful to him.

Next we have to consider the valence of the information—was it positive or negative? In this example, it was very positive. Alternatively, it could be negative: "Do not, under any circumstances, try that restaurant at the corner of Walnut and Broad!" We now have all the ingredients that enable us to define a social contagion process—participants,

---

4 Contagion between people who are far apart happens either because technology is involved (my friend Jeonghye in Seoul emails me a YouTube link), or because people who are normally physically separated get together in person (Jeonghye visits the East Coast for a conference and we watch the clip together).

their locations, their method of communication, and what they actually talk about.

Bouquets, Bricks, and Listening to Your Neighbors (Real and Virtual)

Frictions preventing easy access to information about products and services are rapidly being eliminated through virtual-world communication. Reviews are ubiquitous and inform the majority of purchase decisions related to everything from restaurant choice to vacations to auto sales. One of the first products to attract reviews online was books; in fact, the prolific online reviewer Harriet Klausner has reviewed an astounding 25,000 books herself![5]

Most of us have bought a book online. (Perhaps that's how you purchased this one.) Research shows that reviews are checked in advance for about 75 percent of all purchases. This is not just true for books, but for washing machines, headphones, automobiles, hotels, and so on. You name the product, there's usually at least one review for it and someone who is actively seeking it out.

We'd all like to know what is good, bad, and just plain old mediocre. So it's no surprise that when we buy books online we pay attention to readers' reviews. There are even sites that rate prospective partners and warn against certain individuals! DontDateHimGirl.com is a site where one can "find profiles of men who are alleged cheaters," in addition to "articles on dating and relationships, [offering] advice to help women make better decisions in finding the right man."[6]

So there's a proliferation of information, both negative and positive. Cocktail party fact: the average rating for books sold on Amazon is about 4.1 stars out of a possible 5 stars. Aren't we all rather nice? For whatever reason, reviewers at BarnesAndNoble.com are even a little

---

5   David Streitfeld, "Giving Mom's Book Five Stars? Amazon May Cull Your Review," *New York Times*, December 22, 2012, www.nytimes.com/2012/12/23/technology/amazon-book-reviews-deleted-in-a-purge-aimed-at-manipulation.html?pagewanted=all&_r=2&.

6   Naturally, this kind of site can inflame a few passions. If you want to see more, go to http://reportyourex.com/featured-video-archives/dont-date-him-girl/.

kinder—the average is 4.5 stars, and more than two-thirds of all reviews on the site are 5-star reviews.[7]

On average, it looks as though there is more positive information contained in reviews on the Internet than negative information. Check out Yelp, TripAdvisor, Expedia, and similar sites and apps and you'll see that most of what is said in these places is positive. Negative information is still very powerful, however. Researchers at Yale found that a negative review not only slows the sales of whatever is being reviewed but also tends to reduce the flow of positive reviews.[8]

If we take these findings into account and consider that there is *more* positive information to begin with overall, then, in total, positive word of mouth will be at least as effective as negative word of mouth, if not more so.

Even though reviews are pervasive in the virtual world, which of them get noticed and which are effective depend a lot on the real-world locations of their writers and readers. When reviewers reveal information about themselves, including their location, readers become more willing to trust what's written in their reviews.

We pay more attention to reviews (and reviewers) from our own zip codes than reviews written by those from distant locations.[9]

Why?

Well, the answer lies in one of our favorite (and most important) buzzwords in this book: homophily. Because birds of a feather flock together in the real world, we imagine that those living near us will have similar tastes and preferences as ourselves. So, when we see them weighing in via the virtual world, we trust their opinions. Our real-world neighbors produce the virtual-world information that is most valued by us.

The same principle extends to direct buying and selling in the virtual world as well, as we feel more comfortable dealing online with those who are closer to us in the physical one. You might be able to relate per-

---

7   Judith Chevalier and Dina Mayzlin, "The Effect of Word of Mouth on Sales: Online Book Reviews," *Journal of Marketing Research* 43, no. 3 (August 2006), 345–54.

8   Ibid.

9   Chris Forman, Anindya Ghose, and Batia Wiesenfeld, "Examining the Relationship Between Reviews and Sales: The Role of Reviewer Identity Disclosure in Electronic Markets," *Information Systems Research* 19, no. 3 (September 2008), 291–313.

sonally to this next finding, as most of us have bought and sold things on eBay. It turns out that we all feel a bit happier with the counterparty when that person lives in the same city as we do.[10]

Virtual-World Information and the Competitor Next Door

I suppose it's understandable that we pay more attention to the virtual-world reviews of our real-world neighbors and prefer to buy and sell with them rather than with more distant counterparties. Our real-world neighbors *are* closer, and we feel closer because of that.

But what if review information can't be trusted, whether it's (purportedly) coming from your neck of the woods or not?

By way of background, the *New York Times* reported in 2012 that about one in three online reviews is fake—a number determined by the data-mining expert Bing Liu. And one rather enterprising man, Todd Rutherford, was exposed as making nearly $30,000 a month selling fake reviews online![11]

Interestingly, this sort of fakery in the virtual world can be tied to the presence of certain kinds of real-world neighbors who are not so nice, or at least have an incentive to be untruthful.

Let's focus more specifically on what role the real world could play in giving you a clue as to whether information is truthful or otherwise. Imagine that you own a hotel. Based on what we know so far, this is a business that will attract reviews. And research suggests that you would be wise to pay attention not just to the reviews of the other hotels next to yours in the real world, but also to *who* is managing them (I'll explain why in a moment). Relatedly, if you're a consumer trying to decide whether to stay at a particular hotel, you might like to know a thing or two about the *other* hotels in the neighborhood as well.

A clever study by researchers at the University of Southern Califor-

---

10 Ali Hortacsu, Asis Martinez-Jerez, and Jason Douglas, "The Geography of Trade in Online Transactions: Evidence from eBay and MercadoLibre," *American Economics Journal: Microeconomics* 1, no. 1 (February 2009), 53–74.

11 David Streitfeld, "The Best Book Reviews Money Can Buy," *New York Times*, August 25, 2012, www.nytimes.com/2012/08/26/business/book-reviewers-for-hire-meet-a-demand-for-online-raves.html.

nia and Yale looked at reviews on two sites, TripAdvisor and Expedia, and figured out that certain kinds of online fakery were tied to the real-world locations of the creators and targets of reviews.[12] They also discovered that one of the two sites contains more fakes than the other. Here's a clue as to which. While reviewers on Expedia can write whatever they choose about a hotel, they are offered the option to do so only if their credit card has been connected to a reservation there within the last six months.

That's right, they can only write a review if they've (most likely) stayed in that establishment recently. Reviewers on TripAdvisor, on the other hand, simply have to agree to a kind of honor code.[13]

Talk, as they say, is cheap.

So the researchers had a hunch that the ratings on Expedia were likely to be closer to the "truth" than those on Trip Advisor were, because the raters on Expedia could be verified (more or less) as people who had stayed in specific places, whereas those on Trip Advisor could not be *verified* in the same manner. And that's the important general point from the research that carries over to other types of sites: you should be more trusting of those that have some kind of verification mechanism built in.

The researchers then looked closely at the familiar bar charts of reviews at thousands of properties on the two sites, paying special attention to the lousy (1-star) and outstanding (5-star) reviews. What they were interested in is whether a *specific property*, such as the Le Meridien in San Francisco, had more 1-star ratings on one site than it did on the other.

Cheating and fudging are part of human nature, as the authors themselves note.

Online reviews could, in principle, greatly improve consumers' ability to evaluate products. However, the authenticity of online user reviews

---

12 Dina Mayzlin, Yaniv Dover, and Judith Chevalier, "Promotional Reviews: An Empirical Investigation of Online Review Manipulation," *American Economic Review* (forthcoming).

13 Here's the wording on TripAdvisor's website: "I certify that this review is based on my own experience and is my genuine opinion of this hotel, and that I have no personal or business relationship with this establishment, and have not been offered any incentive or payment originating from the establishment to write this review. I understand that TripAdvisor has a zero-tolerance policy on fake reviews."

remains a concern; firms have an incentive to manufacture positive reviews for their own products and negative reviews for their rivals.[14]

It turns out that the real-world location of sellers plays a key role. Independent owner-operator hotels with more to gain from faking had more 5-star reviews on TripAdvisor than they did on Expedia. This is not to pick on owner-operators but to note that their situations are different from those of large corporate chains, which tend to have management systems in place that are likely to punish cheating. Plus, managers at large chains presumably have less of a personal stake in the success of the business than owner-operators of small hotels do.

Furthermore, hotels that were *neighbors* of these hotels with more incentive to engage in faking had far more 1- and 2-star reviews on TripAdvisor than they did on Expedia. So while your reputation might be made in the virtual world, it certainly matters who you live next to the in the real one.

The general point from the research that carries over to other types of websites is that consumers should be more trusting of reviews with some kind of verification mechanism. Sellers have an incentive to manufacture positive reviews for their own products and negative reviews for their rivals.

The First Time Versus the Next Time

The conversations that take place in a process of social contagion, whether in the real world or in the virtual one, are often very persuasive. They are also worthwhile to consumers because they can dramatically reduce or even eliminate one of the two major frictions—the search friction—which we discussed in chapter 2, RESISTANCE.

As a result, new businesses that reduce frictions can be *extremely* valuable. If you doubt this, remember that TripAdvisor is a public company worth several billion (with a "b") dollars and most of the content is provided by all of us! Also, as we've seen, the real-world locations of the providers and consumers of reviews play a critical role in how the infor-

---

14 Mayzlin, Dover, and Chevalier, "Promotional Reviews."

mation is used and whether it's believable to begin with. This includes the location of neighbors (like Lee), the location of review posters and anonymous counterparties on eBay, and the location of individual sellers relative to their competitors.

So, if my friend Lee tells me about a place down the street that serves great lunches, I'm almost certain to try it out. This raises a few final points (for our purposes at least) about social contagion. What Lee says is very persuasive *before* I gather my own information through experience. This means that conversations are most effective when the person receiving the information has yet to actually try the product or service.

In order for real-world conversations about a product to have an effect on virtual-world buying behavior, the product itself has to deliver. Once you've tried something yourself, you're able to form your own opinion, and the initial word of mouth becomes less relevant. I found this to be true when I studied how people spread information about a national Internet grocery retailer. *Before* someone tried the service, the chance that they would try it was influenced by the number of people around them who had tried it; that is, the more people around them who had used the service, the likelier they were to as well.

There were two reasons for this.

First, there was the homophily effect. Households from the same locations with similar incomes, education levels, and access to stores, were attracted to the Internet seller to the same degree. So, adjacency matters big time, because if one person in a particular area finds an Internet seller attractive, others in that area probably will too. Second, there was a pure contagion effect. People were learning about the service from others around them.

So, new information about a product or service spread through real-world contagion matters most to an individual for his or her *first* purchase. Once a household has tried a new product and experienced it for themselves, the decision of whether to continue purchasing it is relatively unaffected by what the neighbors do.[15]

---

15 For details, see David R. Bell and Sangyoung Song, "Neighborhood Effects and Trial on the Internet: Evidence from Online Grocery Retailing," *Quantitative Marketing and Economics* 5, no. 4 (December 2007), 361–400. This finding is pretty robust. Some other colleagues of mine found similar effects when they looked at physicians prescribing drugs. See Raghuram Iyengar, Christophe Van den Bulte, and Jae Young Lee, "Social Contagion in New

OBSERVATION AMONG ADJACENT INDIVIDUALS

Of course, not every idea that spreads, or every new product that catches on, needs to be powered by conversations. Imitation is a key driver of social contagion too. By that I mean one individual can simply observe another's behavior and start emulating him or her.

Late in 2001 the first iPod was introduced. The device's white color and white earphones in particular created an awesome visual effect. For years, in major cities throughout the United States, Apple put up billboards showing the black silhouette of a listener against the white of the device and the earphones.

In the fall of 2002, I listened to music on it while riding Boston's Red Line train each weekday morning on my way to MIT. It's quite likely that at least some curious fellow riders checked out the iPod as a result of my public use of it. Consumers, like me, inadvertently act as roving ambassadors (I didn't get paid commission), at times inducing other potential customers to buy.

White Toyotas, Empty Restaurants, and Red Bull

A visitor to Tokyo in the late 1980s would quite likely have noticed that most of the cars on the street were white. As it turns out, at that time more than half of all cars sold to private individuals in Tokyo were in fact white. In this particular case there is an externality that reinforced the choice—if everyone is more or less driving a white car, then it might be hard to get a good price for your used lime green Toyota.

I've said a lot about homophily in this book from the get-go—it's just such a useful concept—so let's check one more example. Many of us copy our geographic neighbors when we purchase items that are publically visible. This is especially true for things like cars with resale potential.

Researchers at Ohio State University found that automobile pur-

---

Product Trial and Repeat," (working paper, Wharton School, University of Pennsylvania, Philadelphia, 2013). Contagion happens for initial purchases but tends to dissipate once people have their own information.

chases come in clusters—you're more likely to buy and adopt whatever model your adjacent neighbors do. You coalesce around the brand, features, and so on of their chosen car. The demographics of your neighbors help explain what *you* do![16]

But beyond just "copying" our neighbors, we know from experience that it can make sense to follow the crowd, even when we don't know exactly whom the crowd consists of. For example, if you pass by two restaurants and one is full while the other is empty, which one are you going to go into? You are of course more likely to visit the restaurant with more customers. The crowded room is a "signal" that the one with more customers is likely to be better than the alternative.

The manufacturers of the energy drink Red Bull built upon this logic too. On college campuses in the United States, popular students were given cases of Red Bull to distribute at the parties they hosted. DJs at popular clubs were encouraged to drink Red Bull; bar owners often left the empty cans visible to customers.

Starbucks and Dunkin' Donuts like to see customers take their coffee to go. The cups are visible to others—who might then feel a sudden need for caffeine or a donut. Bonobos pants are famous for their distinctive trim in the back pockets—the pants are easily recognized by fellow aficionados—and often attract the curiosity of others.[17]

Messages from Heaven

As we know, sometimes people learn about new things directly, and sometimes they learn about things from others. But people's propensity to acquire new information through each of these two generic routes depends a lot on their physical location. This principle is illustrated in a very clever experiment carried out in Birmingham, Alabama, in the 1950s.[18]

---

16 Sha Yang and Greg Allenby, "Modeling Interdependent Consumer Preferences," *Journal of Marketing Research* 40, no. 3 (August 2003), 282–94.

17 You might like to try the following experiment: buy a pair of pants from Bonobos.com and see if anyone notices (and comments on) the pocket trim!

18 See Ørjar Øyen and Melvin De Fleur, "The Spatial Diffusion of an Airborne Leaflet Message," *American Journal of Sociology* 59, no. 2 (September 1953), 144–49.

Technologies evolve more quickly than fundamental human behaviors do so sometimes it's good to revisit these classic findings!

In the study, over 300,000 leaflets (about one per resident) were dropped on the city from a plane. The leaflet contained a message asking anyone who came across it to fill it out and mail it back. About 7 percent of the leaflets (just under 20,000) were mailed back to the experimenters, which is a pretty decent response rate.

Of the responses, 55 percent were from physical diffusion — i.e., someone picked up a leaflet, filled it in, and mailed it back. The remaining 45 percent of the responses were from so-called social diffusion. This means that the respondent got the leaflet from someone else first. So some people saw the leaflets and acted on them directly, while others passed them along to friends, who complied with the request.

A related experiment in Seattle produced a complementary insight. The people who filled in the leaflets directly tended to live right underneath the places where the drops had occurred, whereas the people who learned about the leaflets socially tended to live farther from where the leaflets had been dropped.

So in the real world, proximity and social transmission go hand in hand. That's why virtual-world products and services can benefit tremendously from real-world adjacencies among customers.

In chapter 6 (TOPOGRAPHY) I'll explain in a bit more detail how social transmission works in the virtual world, where the relevance and value of virtual-world information for recipients depends, in part, on where the senders and recipients actually live, and how similar their respective locations are to each other.

The Mechanics of Adjacency

The famous statistician George Box once said, "Essentially, all models are wrong, but some are useful."[19] That's the spirit in which I approach things in this section. We're going to look at some simple yet powerful models that will give you a way of thinking about adjacency that is both

---

19 George Box and Norman Draper, *Empirical Model Building and Response Surfaces* (New York: John Wiley & Sons, 1987).

practically useful and also consistent with rigorous academic research. I'm going to discuss adjacency relationships between zip codes (for ease of illustration), but what I show below applies equally to relationships between individuals as well. To make this clear I'll provide a few examples along the way.

ADJACENCY AMONG ZIP CODES IN A CLUSTER

In order to see how adjacency in either the real or virtual world leads to particular patterns of behavior, we need to understand the most basic form of adjacent relationship.

Again, the concept that I elaborate on below applies equally to almost any unit of analysis—people, zip codes, nodes in a network, and so on—but I am going to focus on zip codes. This book is, after all, about location.

The average zip code in the United States shares a boundary with about five other zip codes. Zip codes adjacent to lakes or oceans (or Canada or Mexico) have fewer shared boundaries; those in dense metropolitan areas have a greater number. What follows is a little technical, but bear with me. The concepts below are helpful and enlightening in our quest to understand how real-world adjacency fuels growth for virtual-world sellers.

Figure 3.1 on the next page forms the basis of our example; it shows four different zip codes in a cluster (on the left-hand side) as well as some other information.

Connecting Zips to Make a Neighborhood

Zip code number 1 shares a border with number 2 and number 3. Zip code number 2 shares a boundary with all three other zip codes, as does zip code number 3. Zip code number 4, like zip code number 1, is connected only to numbers 2 and 3.

So, how can we represent the set of relationships in this neighborhood cluster?

Well, since there are four zip codes, we will create a matrix with four

Figure 3.1

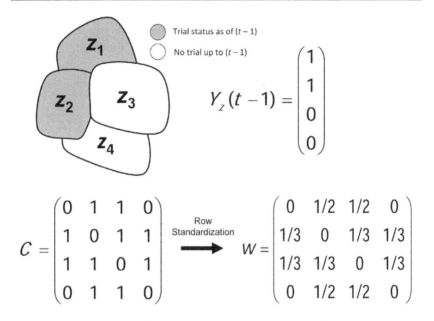

rows (one for each zip code) and four columns (one for each zip code that a zip code can be connected to). There are 16 (4×4) cells in this matrix, one for every possible connection among zip codes. By convention, all the "diagonal" entries in the matrix (i.e., row 1, column 1; row 2, column 2), have a zero in them. This just means that each zip code is not "connected" to itself.

That sounds rather sensible, doesn't it?

To understand how adjacency relates to influence, let's focus on row number 1, the row for zip code number 1.

The first entry (row 1, column 1) contains a zero because of the convention that all diagonal elements are zero, i.e., that zip code number 1 is not connected to itself. Next, columns 2 and 3 contain a one. This is because zip code number 1 is connected to both zip code number 2 and zip code number 3. Finally, as you may have guessed, column 4 contains a zero because zip codes number 1 and number 4 are not connected to each other.

The matrix summarizing all of the relationships among the four zip codes is shown at the bottom left of figure 3.1. This is a pretty simple association matrix, or contiguity matrix. The entry in a cell is a zero if the pair of zip codes indicated by that cell don't share a boundary, and it's a one if they do.

In simple terms, the matrix shows what zip codes are contiguous with, or adjacent to, which other ones. Even though I've focused on zip codes, you can see how this kind of idea could apply to some other entity, or unit of analysis.

Like people, for instance.

Imagine that we're studying four people on Facebook and trying to figure out who might be influencing whom. Applying this model, we will say that the four people are Alyssa (number 1), Brent (number 2), Carolyn (number 3), and Daniel (number 4). Replacing zip codes 1 through 4 in figure 3.1 with people, we could say that Alyssa and Daniel don't know each other, but Brent and Carolyn know everyone.

ADJACENCY AND INFLUENCE

So now that we have a way to define adjacent or neighboring zip codes (or adjacent people in a social network), I'd like to illustrate some different ways to measure how much influence is being brought to bear on a particular zip code (or person) by adjacent ones.

Let's look back at figure 3.1.

At the top left of the figure, zip codes 1 and 2 are shaded gray. The reason for this is that at the end of the last observation period (time "$t-1$"), the focal activity—say, buying groceries online—had already occurred at that location. Zip codes 3 and 4 are not shaded in, because online shopping has yet to take place in either area. This same information is shown in the vector to the right of figure 3.1 as well, where a one indicates that the activity we're interested in *has* occurred in the first two zip codes and a zero indicates that it *has not* in the last two. (The vector has four rows, one for each of the four zip codes.)

Let's take zip code 3, one of the zip codes for which we are still waiting for the activity to occur, and try to understand how much "pressure" from adjacency will be applied to it. There are three adjacent zip codes — numbers 1, 2, and 4 — and for our purposes, these are the ones that have the ability to influence what goes on in zip code number 3.[20] For now, we are focused on physical relationships and direct influence, so only adjoining zip codes can influence each other.

The simplest assumption we could make is that each zip code is impacted in equal proportion by whatever neighbors it has. Zip code number 3 has three neighbors. So, one starting point is that each neighbor has a 33 percent influence on what goes on there. Zip code number 4, on the other hand, has two direct neighbors (numbers 2 and 3), so they each exert an influence equal to 50 percent.

Figure 3.1 puts this "equal influence" concept into action. If you look closely at the bottom right of the figure, you'll notice that the rows of the standardized contiguity matrix always add up to one. This is intuitive: the total amount of influence to be exerted on any one location by the adjacent neighboring locations is 100 percent exactly, and no more.

Influence Relationships

There are many other ways that we could specify the influence relationships. Imagine that influence from one zip code to another is proportional to the number of people who live in the influencing zip codes. Let's say that zip code number 2 has four times the population of zip code number 3. To reflect this, we could replace the ½, ½, entries that are currently in row 4 of figure 3.1 with ⅘, and ⅕. Alternative ways of specifying influence relationships include the driving distances between the centers of the zip codes, the relative population sizes, and so on. If we're talking about people, the degree of influence could be related to wealth, status, number of friends, and so on.

Technical details aside, we now have a very important concept in place for exploring and quantifying how searching, shopping, and selling in the virtual world are affected by adjacencies that exist in the

---

20 Technically, this is called influence by "first-order contiguity." Through "second-order contiguity," zip code 4 could influence zip code 3, which in turn could influence zip code 1.

real world.[21] We've come up with a structured way to relate different elements of the *real* world—in this case, locations—to each other, and then connect them to activities that occur in the *virtual* world.

For example, because we know that "adjacent" people imitate and talk to each other, this means that when some *virtual-world* activity, like posting up on Pinterest or buying razors from Harrys.com, starts taking hold in a particular real-world location (such as PA 19104), we have some way of figuring out where it is likely to go next.

Imagine, for example, that we saw Harrys.com shaving kits catching on like wildfire in zip codes numbers 1 and 2. Because of the close physical association (proximity) between zip codes numbers 3 and the neighbors (numbers 1 and 2), we might expect that it won't be long before sales occur in zip code number 3.

Here's the important takeaway.

Physical neighborhoods can be defined not only in terms of their characteristics but also *spatially* and *in relation* to one another. Because people who live in immediate neighborhood clusters are also likely to be similar to each other in specific ways, it's not that hard to imagine ideas, fads, and trends spreading among them.

In fact, there are a variety of patterns that we might expect to see, depending on the type of product or service being considered.

Characterizing Locations

Before I explain in detail how the patterns of spreading happen, let's examine a little more closely the ways to characterize physical neighborhoods.

THE PHYSICAL NEIGHBORHOOD

The neighborhood is where collections of individuals, with similar tastes and interests, cluster together and where they interact with each

---

21 If you are curious about the technical details, take a look at Bell and Song, "Neighborhood Effects and Trial on the Internet."

other. The interaction might be rather intimate—a chat after work about the week's projects—or rather incidental. Incidental interaction happens in bars, coffee shops, and even the local supermarket. These interactions are opportunities to learn about new products, services, and ideas. And as we just saw, the learning happens through interaction or observation.

Neighborhood Features and Interaction

The structure of our physical neighborhood helps determine how information spreads through adjacent locations and how likely interaction among individuals is to begin with.

Three things are critical.

First, physical population density—the more people there are, the more opportunities there are for incidental contact. The subway is more crowded (even the fact that there is a subway means that density has reached some kind of threshold); there are more people circulating in bars, and more people walking on the street.

Second, when there are more people in your neighborhood, there are more offline establishments where interaction can occur. As noted in chapter 1, this is a bit of a chicken and egg situation too—more people bring forth more stores; in turn, more stores and offline services may make a location more desirable.

Third, the people themselves are important to consider. Some communities are very homogenous, others more diverse. The similarity among the residents themselves matters because a more diverse neighborhood will reflect more disparate tastes and preferences. An individual living in a diverse neighborhood will therefore be exposed to more new things—more variety in everything from food to clothes, and from bars to sit-down restaurants.

On the other hand, neighborhood cohesion is usually higher when residents are more similar. If all of the residents are middle-aged Catholics with children, their neighborhood should contain a fair number of schools and churches. The residents may also share political affiliations, favorite foods, and sports teams.

As mentioned in chapter 1, GEOGRAPHY, the cohesiveness of a neighborhood is reflected in the amount of social capital that has accumulated there.[22] Recall that, in simple terms, social capital captures how much residents trust each other and how often they interact. Some neighborhoods have high social capital—people interact frequently, get along well, and generally look out for each other. In other neighborhoods, it's very much every man for himself!

Tagging the Real World with Zip Codes

So let's define what we mean by "neighborhood." Determining where a neighborhood begins and ends is not always easy. As a matter of convenience more than anything else, and of course for consistency with figure 3.1, I'll define neighborhoods by zip code.[23]

There are more than forty thousand zip codes in the United States, and while this is not always a perfect measure of a neighborhood, the zip code is certainly a useful one thanks to the infrastructure that's grown up around it. Marketers, insurance companies, credit agencies, and even political parties all target individual households on the basis of the zip codes in which they live.

Some zip codes are even aspirational—who wouldn't want to at least visit CA 90210? Zip code numbers get larger as one moves from the eastern states, from, say, 02142 in Cambridge, Massachusetts, (home to the Sloan School of Management) to 90024 in Westwood, California (home to UCLA). They also tend to get bigger in area.

Anyway, the point is not that everyone who lives in MA 02142 or CA 90024 is the same, but rather that they share similar characteristics (such as education and income levels), and more subtly, that they are likely to share preferences too. For example, the residents of Cambridge, Massachusetts, might like the Boston Red Sox, four distinct seasons, and (perhaps) higher education a bit more than the residents

---

22 See Robert Putnam, *Bowling Alone: The Collapse and Revival of American Community* (New York: Simon & Schuster, 2000); http://bowlingalone.com/.

23 Zip codes (and their direct analogs in other countries) have their origins in the postal system. They started out as a way to improve efficiency in sorting and sending mail.

of Westwood, California, do. The latter might quite likely favor the Lakers, year-round sunshine, and cultural pursuits related to movies. The people who live in MA 02141 are more likely to be similar to those who live in the neighboring location MA 02142 than to those who live in CA 90025.

Once we know a bit about who lives in a zip code and what's there in terms of offline infrastructure (stores, bars, restaurants, and so on) we have a great base from which to understand what the residents of that zip code will do online. The offline options tell us a lot about what the residents might like to do, and how and where they interact.

Entire industries, starting with the government census, are built up around collecting data about zip codes. And just as important, everyone who shops or sells on the Internet either gives out or receives zip code information in the form of billing and shipping addresses.

So, we have a "unit of analysis," the zip code, that is both well defined and widely used. These are very attractive properties for building models and ideas that explain how the real and virtual worlds interact. The fact that zip codes are something of an arbitrary measure is OK—they are more than good enough.

Neighborhood Effects in Action

So far I've explained what adjacency means for homophily and influence, so it's time to put these concepts to work.

TRADING AREAS AND THE GRAVITY PRINCIPLE

When we start copying our neighbors and sharing ideas with them, virtual-world sellers can expect very pronounced patterns of demand to emerge. I'll illustrate the culmination of everything I've discussed so far with a very basic example—grocery shopping—as that's something that we can all relate to.

Prior to the existence of the Internet we all visited local stores for our groceries. In fact, even *after* the Internet came along, most of us still visit local stores. Joost van der Laan at RetailEconomics.com reports that in 2012, less than 1 percent of grocery retail in the United States was done online.[24]

There's mounting optimism about the future of grocery retail in the virtual world (in the introduction I noted that Amazon Fresh is moving aggressively in this space), but there is still some naysaying as well. As my friend and colleague Pete Fader might say, perhaps there's a good reason why the percentage of groceries bought online in 2012 is "close to what it was in 1812."

Down to Basics: Shopping for Groceries in the Real and Virtual Worlds

The average family in the United States regularly visits two to three supermarkets for food, cleaning products, and household supplies and supermarkets are great examples of the trading area concept.

A trading area is just a geographic unit that contains all the customers of a particular store (or restaurant, movie theater, car wash, etc.). All trading areas are subject to, and defined by, gravity. For customers who live close by, the pull is strong. When a customer lives too far away, a seller has no ability to attract him or her.

Take the supermarket chain Dominick's Finer Foods in Chicago. Dominick's has a store in the zip code IL 60603 that draws customers from seventy-two different zip codes.

Not surprisingly, all of them are from Illinois. In fact, there aren't even any customers coming from across town in Chicago, let alone from, say, St. Louis. Of course, we all know this intuitively, but I am pushing the point a bit just to help show the contrast with what happens online.

Because the gravitational pull that a store has over you weakens the farther away you are from it, the implicit and actual costs of traveling to a store increase the farther away you are from it too.

It takes more time, more gas, more hassle.

Unfortunately, the benefits (low prices, great selection, nice service) *do not* change with distance from the store. They aren't affected by grav-

---

24 Joost W. van der Laan, "Online Grocery Retailing is a Tricky Business," RetailEconomics, http://retaileconomics.com/online-grocery-retailing/.

ity at all. Dominick's won't say to a customer: "Wow, you drove all the way from the other side of Chicago just to shop here—let me give you a 50 percent discount on everything, and please allow our staff to fill your cart while you enjoy a nice cup of coffee."

If costs increase with distance but benefits don't, then the cost-benefit equation for a particular seller becomes more and more bleak the farther away you are. Hence, you're less likely to visit an offline store the farther away it is, all else being equal. As I'll show in a moment, this same principle governs attraction for virtual-world stores too, and is what makes real-world adjacencies so important for virtual-world sellers.

So now that we understand the trading area for a regular store, and why it looks the way that it does, we can start to comprehend how things differ for an Internet store, and why adjacency in the real world matters for sales in the virtual one. We'll stick with groceries, just to keep things simple, but the principle applies much more generally.

In May 1997 Ari Sabah and his colleagues founded Netgrocer.com, with the motto "Groceries and more, delivered straight to your door!" Netgrocer.com is headquartered in New Jersey and certainly didn't survive the Internet boom and bust by serving only the sixty to seventy or so zip codes centered on NJ 07346. The trading area for Netgrocer .com was and is far different from that of Dominick's Finer Foods in IL 60603. Netgrocer.com can serve customers in any zip code in the United States, as long as it has the means to ship products there.[25]

Back in May 1997, its first month of operations, Netgrocer.com enticed customers from thirty-four different zip codes.

That's right, in the first month its trading area covered only thirty-four zip codes—a bit less than half the number served by Dominick's Finer Foods in Chicago.

Now let's roll things forward a bit.

After about three and half years in business (by January 2001), Netgrocer.com had served customers in more than eighteen thousand

25 Netgrocer.com ships internationally now as well. This just underscores the point that its trading area is limited only by its ability to ship product (typically through third-party experts like UPS or FedEx).

zip codes![26] Now, I don't mean that it was selling to customers in all eighteen thousand zip codes every single week or month, but *at some point* in the company's brief history, customers had been served in all of those places.

More interesting, though, than the sheer size of Netgrocer.com's trading area is the way in which it has developed over time and across locations. Figure 3.2 shows the trading area expanding rapidly over a period of about three years. While this figure captures the growth of the trading area, it doesn't reveal the mechanism of adjacency that is underlying it. So, let's dig into the details and see how real-world adjacency helps virtual-world sellers grow.

Adjacency and Diffusion

Now, even though Netgrocer.com had served no more than a few hundred zip codes by the end of July 1997, in the subsequent months, numerous others were added to its trading area. Did these new zip codes just join the trading area randomly, or was there some kind of pattern? If the new zip codes had in fact joined "randomly," we should expect to see them scattered evenly throughout the United States. Or was the chance that a zip code joined the trading area potentially related to its size—zip codes with more people attracting more new customers—or to some other factor such as wealth or education level?

What actually happened can be seen in the detail in figure 3.3.

The six panels in the figure are paired snapshots of the East (right panel) and West (left panel) Coasts of the United States and show new zip codes arriving into the trading area every month. Darkened areas have customers, and the first panel pair in the figure illustrates the pattern early on in the life of Netgrocer.com. The second and third pairs show how things evolved with time.

Now, if you look closely, you will see that new zip codes with customers in later time periods are more likely to be locations that are contiguous with other zip codes that *already had* customers.

---

26 Again, if you want to read the whole story, see Bell and Song, "Neighborhood Effects and Trial on the Internet."

Figure 3.2

a Locations with Customers as of December 1997

b Locations with Customers as of December 1998

c Locations with Customers as of December 1999

d Locations with Customers as of December 2000

Figure 3.3

Locations with Customers as of June 1997

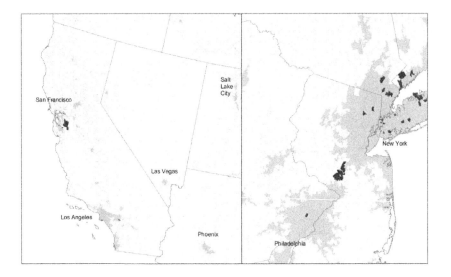

Locations with Customers as of September 1997

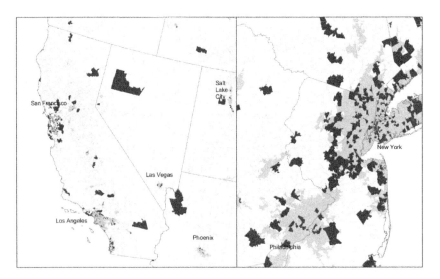

Locations with Customers as of December 1997

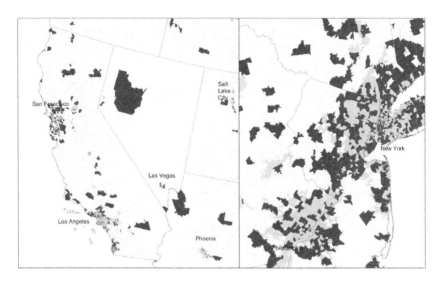

What you see here on a small scale was in fact what occurred throughout the *entire* country. New customers popped up in areas adjacent to areas that already had customers.

"Wait!" you say. "Of course we see this pattern. It's explained by homophily, that old 'birds of a feather flock together' thing! People that live close by each other in the real world share characteristics and tastes, and access to offline retail stores, so that's why they are drawn to virtual-world seller Netgrocer.com at roughly the same time."

And you're (partly) right.

When we looked closely and rigorously at the data through a statistical analysis, we found that zip codes with more affluent and educated customers were indeed likelier to see trials of Netgrocer.com sooner than other zip codes were. We also found that Netgrocer.com did better in locations where people had to travel farther to reach large discounters and warehouse clubs. So when offline access to stores was not so good, shoppers were more likely to shop online.

So yes, the characteristics of residents matter, and ease of access to local offline stores does as well. Everything we've seen in chapters 1 and 2 (GEOGRAPHY and RESISTANCE) would have predicted this. People with similar tastes and profiles have clustered into contiguous locations, and locations differ in the amount of friction involved in accessing off-line stores.

But there's another force at work in the patterns I just showed you in figures 3.2 and 3.3. As Neil Young might say, "there is more to the picture (than meets the eye)."[27]

Adjacency and Contagion

The second force relates to the "pressure" story that I mentioned earlier and showed in Figure 3.1. Relating the actual patterns seen in Netgrocer .com data to the example—if zip code number 3 is connected to zip codes number 1 and 2, and people in both of these zip codes have already started using Netgrocer.com, chances are it's only a matter of time before someone in zip code number 3 does as well.

This second effect—contagion resulting from adjacency—proved very robust in the case of Netgrocer.com. First-time orders from new customers were more likely to show up in a zip code when there had been previous orders by other customers in contiguous zip codes.

This effect persisted even after accounting for the "birds of a feather" effect, or the tendency of co-located people, such as those in the same zip code, to behave similarly. So holding all else constant, as our economist friends might say (and it *is* important to do that), there are very strong *real-world* contagion dynamics that create these demand-spreading patterns for *virtual-world* sellers.

In short, the trading area for Netgrocer.com expanded systematically. Once a few customers sprouted up somewhere, their neighbors soon joined them. This kind of contagion resulting from real-world adjacency has shown up in the data of every virtual-world seller that I've looked at.[28] In chapter 4, VICINITY, I'll look more closely at where customers pop up to begin with, expand the idea of "proximity," and also examine some of the best ways to "seed" locations with new cus-

---

27 And perhaps more prescriptively, "It's better to burn out, than it is to rust." Hey hey, my my indeed.

28 Adjacency delivers the main, or "first-order," effect of contagion, and the mechanisms of vicinity and isolation create some further nuances. I discuss these in chapters 4 and 5 respectively.

tomers. Virtual-world businesses benefit tremendously from real-world adjacencies among customers and neighborhoods. Intelligent sellers understand this and do their best to cultivate activity that leverages adjacencies.

Tying Things Down With A Little Bit of History: Cooling Off in Philadelphia

Perhaps we shouldn't be too surprised by the ubiquity of real-world adjacency causing contagion in the virtual world. After all, local copying, chatter, and emulation have all been around for a long time in the real world.

A classic study from back in the 1950s (and from Philadelphia to boot) further supports the point by demonstrating the reinforcing roles of conversation and visual observation when adjacent individuals copy each other's behavior. The researchers found clustering patterns when examining how residents of Philadelphia neighborhoods adopted air conditioners.[29]

Air conditioners were relatively new at the time, so they were likely to be the subject of conversation. In addition, they protrude from houses, so it's pretty easy for others to see them. Conversations and observations worked together to generate the clustered diffusion patterns observed by the researchers.

In the same way, it's possible for two neighbors to talk about Bonobos .com, Harrys.com, WarbyParker.com, or any other virtual-world business. Alternatively, someone previously unfamiliar with these sellers might encounter shipping boxes in a neighbor's doorway or in the mailroom at the office, and later visit the site.

Interestingly, contagion driven by adjacency is getting more pronounced as we all move from "fixed" Internet devices (like laptops) to mobile devices (like tablets and smartphones). This is because of something my friend Rob Coneybeer at Shasta Ventures calls "show and tell". When I discover a new site, or app, or YouTube video, I can now easily

---

29 William H. Whyte, Jr, "The Web of Word of Mouth," *Fortune,* 50 (November 1954), 140–43.

show it to you on my iPhone while we chat and have coffee. More about this in chapter 6, TOPOGRAPHY.

Summary

Great pairings are powerful, from Bonnie and Clyde to bacon and eggs. So, too, with the two great benefits of adjacency—homophily and influence. Homophily implies that people who live next to each other share characteristics and circumstances, and so make similar trade-offs, and can be drawn to use similar virtual-world products and services. When they communicate and emulate, influence happens.

Homophily can be leveraged, but influence can be fanned. That's why it's critical for virtual-world sellers to consider how to make their products and services socially visible. It was no accident that my Soap .com boxes came in vibrant mixed colors like teal, orange, chocolate, and magenta, with "Soap.com" written on them in white letters. If your workplace "family" is bigger than your family at home, then your virtual-world seller should encourage you to get your items shipped to your office as well. That means more exposure—my Wharton colleagues have seen many of my orders over the years!

In the virtual world, most sellers have unlimited reach—through a whole country, or perhaps even the entire world—yet their sales don't occur just anywhere. The patterns of demand that emerge when a seller conquers an "unlimited market" have special properties. They are rooted in adjacency, as new buyers spring up in areas contiguous with ones that have buyers already.

Adjacency rules. You'll succeed when you seed it and let proximity power demand.

Four

VICINITY

Ties That Bind: Physical Distance, Social Distance, and the Spatial Long Tail

VI·CIN·I·TY *n.*
The state of being near in space or in relationship; proximity.

In chapter 3, ADJACENCY, we looked at how real-world adjacencies influence how virtual-world behaviors spread among people and communities that are physically close to each other.

We also saw that the path of the spreading is very predictable. It looks a bit like a contagious disease, moving from one adjacent person to the next, one neighborhood to the next, and so on.

There are two very important concepts that provide the underlying reasons for this.

So important, in fact, that I have to mention them again.

Concept number one is (once again) homophily, or the "birds of a feather flock together" idea. Since my friend Phil and I share tastes, preferences, and characteristics, we have ended up living in apartments in the same neighborhood. We live in apartments in Philadelphia, PA 19123, and Philadelphia, PA 19124, respectively.

By the Tiebout sorting principle, Phil and I performed cost-benefit calculations for a variety of locations and ended up coming to similar conclusions. That is, that our proximate zip codes are the best places for us to live at the moment.

But due to our choice of where to live, we share more than just traits and preferences. We are also exposed to the same real-world constraints (or face the same RESISTANCE to getting what we want as discussed in chapter 2). Our similarities in terms of characteristics, preferences, and constraints lead us to have common patterns of use for all that is available to us in the virtual world.

The second concept is influence. When people are in close proximity, there's always the possibility for influence. Your neighbor tells you about a new local restaurant or travel app or Internet fashion website. Or maybe you see a Soap.com box piled on top of the trash in your apartment building and decide to check out the website.

So, influence operates either through conversations or through direct observation. As mobile Internet devices (smart phones and tablets) proliferate, they create opportunities for ideas to be shared and demonstrated at the same time. Sitting in a café, I can tell my friend about the Nest (www.nest.com) thermostat on my wall at home, while showing him how I control it via my iPhone.

Homophily and influence result from, and are made possible by, adjacency. But it turns out that there is more to the idea of adjacency than just physical proximity. That's what this chapter is about—there are many other people out there like you, perhaps hundreds or even thousands of miles away, yet they share many things in common with you. In short, they are in the same *vicinity*, in market terms, even though they are not adjacent in any physical sense.

Physical Distance and Social Distance in the Real World

In the real world, we've all made a decision about where to live. That decision is fairly stable and typically has a long "shelf life," even among very mobile people like the Americans.

By "stable," I mean that many of us move only every few years, and it would be unusual for someone to move every few months (unless he or she were on the run!). Either consciously, through careful calculation, or through some feeling of affinity for a location, we've most likely ended up in a neighborhood with people who are quite like us. Our profiles and that of our families are pretty close to those of the other people in our building, street, and zip code.

NEIGHBOR SEE, NEIGHBOR DO

Since our neighbors are physically close, there is a good chance that we'll bump into them — in the street, the supermarket, the lobby, or perhaps at church on Sunday. When this happens, we hear about what they are up to, and we see what they're doing.

Closeness in terms of physical proximity allows people who are already quite similar to one another to start sharing and talking about things. This leads to the patterns of real- and virtual-world diffusion that we saw in chapter 3, ADJACENCY. These patterns are remarkably robust and occur for all kinds of products.

In contemporary society, the desire to "keep up with the Joneses" is common and no doubt plays a role in some of the emulation we observe among neighbors. A study conducted by researchers at the University of Chicago found that the greater the proportion of neighbors who had computers was, the more likely individual households who didn't already have one were to buy one.[1]

And it didn't just stop there.

The researchers also found that the brand of computers owned by the neighbors seems to impact the brand we own too. For the most part — there are always some contrarian souls who like to stand out — most of us are more conformist than perhaps we would care to admit.

This is interesting, because it's one of those "all else being equal" find-

---

[1]   Austan Goolsbee and Peter Klenow, "Evidence of Learning and Network Externalities in the Diffusion of Home Computers," *Journal of Law and Economics* 45, no. 2 (October 2002), 317–43.

ings. That is, if we took two neighborhoods that were identical in all respects (population size, income, education levels, and so on), the cascading effect of emulation means that the neighborhood with the higher current penetration of computers would be the one with the higher future penetration too.

The effect on sales—whether for local computer stores or online merchants—is driven simply by the fact that people who live close to each other share tastes and also influence one another.

Surprisingly, this kind of emulation is not only seen in individual decisions but also in those made by corporations as well. One study by researchers at UCLA and Duke found that large retail chains and competitors tend to copy each other's products as soon as they debut.[2] If Safeway supermarkets in Los Angeles just launched DJ's new frozen pizza with artichokes, then it certainly won't be long until Ralphs supermarkets do as well.

Hold the extra cheese!

As we saw in the previous chapter, real-world proximity among individuals explains a lot of real- and virtual-world activity—how information is shared and used, what is bought online, and so on. Social scientists of all stripes (economists, psychologists, and sociologists) necessarily spend a lot of time thinking about distance. And they've concluded that there is much more to distance than just its physical aspect.

SPRINGFIELD, ILLINOIS, VERSUS LOS ANGELES, CALIFORNIA

A study conducted over thirty-five years ago provides a very nice insight into some alternative meanings of distance. It's also a great starting point for our examination of the concept of vicinity.

Back in 1978, Claude Fischer published an article titled "Urban-to-Rural Diffusion of Opinions in Contemporary America" in the *American Journal of Sociology*.[3] In it, Fischer argued that a randomly selected

---

2 Bart Bronnenberg and Carl Mela, "Market Roll-Out and Retailer Adoption of New Brands," *Marketing Science* 23, no. 4 (November 2004), 500–518.

3 Claude Fischer, "Urban-to-Rural Diffusion of Opinions in Contemporary America," *American Journal of Sociology* 84, no. 1 (July 1978), 151–59.

resident of Chicago had a greater chance of coming into contact with someone from Los Angeles than with someone from Springfield, even though Springfield is much closer to Chicago than Los Angeles is. In fact, the distance between Los Angeles and Chicago (about two thousand miles) is approximately ten times as great as the distance between Springfield and Chicago (about two hundred miles).

Why did Fischer argue the Chicagoan and the Angeleno were more likely to meet?

Even though the *physical* distance from Chicago to Springfield is about one tenth of the distance to Los Angeles, the *social distance* between Chicago and Springfield is much *greater* than it is between Los Angeles and Chicago. As we go through the chapter, I'll explain more about what social distance actually is. Suffice it to say, just because locations are separated whopping physical distances, it doesn't mean that they won't behave the same way when it comes to adopting new products and services. Also, thanks to the Internet, a large physical distance between locations no longer precludes influence or interaction flowing between them.

Now let's relate this to what we observed with Netgrocer.com sales in chapter 3, ADJACENCY. Imagine that you're running an Internet retailer and you find that you have strong sales in parts of Chicago. Based on our earlier discussion, you'd expect some kind of "spillover" into relatively close geographic areas, but now, based on a different notion of "similarity," you might expect things to pick up in Los Angeles as well. (I'll say more about the details in a moment.)

THE BOY NEXT DOOR (LITERALLY AND METAPHORICALLY)

Research has also shown that in many contexts, physical and social proximity can substitute for each other. One clever example examined the behavior of entrepreneurs and inventors.

What does this mean, exactly?

Well, first of all, if you and I are both running start-ups and working on the same city block, or even better yet, in the same incubator, we can benefit from sharing information with each other and helping each other out. Adjacency to the fore again!

It's no surprise that many start-up incubators do in fact set themselves up this way. Take Launchpad LA, for example, a start-up incubator in Los Angeles where I serve as a mentor. The incoming class shares a physical office space. In fall 2012 the group was incredibly diverse — its members were launching everything from awesome shoes (www.milk andhoneyshoes.com) to better ways to enjoy golf (www.swingbyswing .com).

Now imagine that two people who could benefit from interaction with each other live quite some distance apart but share a common and tightly connected cultural background. What is surprising is that a strong cultural similarity can *substitute* or make up for a lack of physical closeness.

My friend Drake and I both immigrated to the United States from New Zealand and share a strong cultural identity and background. Even though he lives in Los Angeles and I mostly live in Philadelphia, we are able to work closely together on his start-up. Our shared cultural experience — our high degree of *similarity* in this one important dimension — makes up for the fact that we are physically separated.

As noted in chapter 3 (ADJACENCY), marketing researchers at Ohio State University were interested in whether our auto purchases are connected to the auto purchases made by those around us. They found that households living in relatively close proximity to each other were more likely to own the same model of car (and even the same color).[4]

Now, this might be expected to some extent — if I see a street full of Volvos I might just be more likely to buy one myself, perhaps out of the desire to conform, or perhaps just because of the exposure I've had to the brand. The important principle uncovered in the study is that *demographic similarity* (as well as *geographic proximity*) has a big effect on car choice as well. People pay attention not only to what kind of cars are on the block, but also to what kind of cars people *like themselves* are driving, regardless of where they saw the car.

So there is quite a bit of evidence indicating that similarity, more than distance alone, matters a lot for choices and behaviors. As I will

---

4   Sha Yang and Greg Allenby, "Modeling Interdependent Consumer Preferences," *Journal of Marketing Research* 40, no. 3 (August 2003), 282–94.

show shortly, thanks to the virtual world of the Internet, individuals sharing characteristics, circumstances, and preferences can be bound together more easily than ever before.

Let's look at one last example, which shows that what's true for individuals and neighborhoods is, surprisingly, even applicable to entire organizations operating in different countries.

Researchers at UCLA looked at the cross-national adoption of something called ISO 9000 and something else called ISO 14000.[5] These are certifications for organizational management and environmental management systems.[6]

The authors of this study wanted to know if there was any pattern in how these certifications were obtained by companies over time. In line with our earlier discussion in chapter 3 (ADJACENCY), they found that physical proximity played a very important role for both certifications.

Companies were more likely to obtain them when proximate companies had already done so. So, the basic concept of adjacency extends beyond just individuals and neighborhoods to corporate entities as well.

At the same time, two other forces pointed to the fact that certifying companies were in the same *vicinity* as each other as well. First, individual companies were more likely to obtain management standard certification (ISO 9000) when other companies with similar trading patterns had already done so. So, there was a kind of "homophily" around trading patterns, independent of the physical location of the companies. Second, companies sought environmental certification (ISO 14000) when other early adopter companies in "culturally similar" countries had already done so.

Hence, distance and proximity in the real world can be based on both geographic and nongeographic (demographic, cultural, and economic) considerations. So, if we want to understand how individual buyers and sellers will cluster in the same virtual-world vicinity, we need to take all of these factors into account.

---

5   Paulo Albuquerque, Bart J. Bronnenberg, and Charles Corbett, "A Spatio-Temporal Analysis of Global Diffusion of ISO 9000 and ISO 14000 Certification," *Management Science* 53, no. 3 (March 2007), 451–68.

6   *Wikipedia*, s.v. "ISO 9000," last modified October 27, 2013, http://en.wikipedia.org/wiki/ISO_9000.

Distance in the Virtual World

In chapter 2, RESISTANCE, I explained that the physical distance between consumers and suppliers, counterintuitively, matters a lot not only for the flow of goods in the real world but also for the consumption of content in the virtual one. Rugby lovers in Philadelphia, all else being equal, consume more rugby content from South African sites than from Australian ones.

The novel fact is that this is true even when the content is pretty much identical — everything else held constant. The data also show that US consumers, for example, don't like to "travel" too far for their pornography (Canadian sites are preferred).

Of course, it's no surprise that when we start thinking about people and neighborhoods deemed to be in close proximity in the real world, we usually begin by thinking about geography. That is, "close proximity" usually means "geographically close" as a starting point. But as we've seen, we can also get a lot of mileage from thinking about clusters of individuals or clusters of locations that share characteristics (such as age, income, education, occupation, landscape, and amenities) also as being in the same vicinity.

Vicinity in the virtual world can be defined either by the preferences and tastes of community members in a virtual neighborhood or, as in the real world, by their characteristics. However, in the virtual world it becomes possible for individuals to become more narrow and circumscribed in their interests. That is, they can seek out others who share their tastes (independent of distance), form bonds, and spend a good deal of time interacting online.

Whether this is a good thing for buyers, sellers, or even society as a whole is an interesting topic for debate.

PROPERTIES OF THE VIRTUAL NEIGHBORHOOD

Common Interests and Disparate Locations

Affiliations can be defined in lots of different ways. The worldwide readership of RugbyHeaven.com and Rugby365.com is made of affiliate groups based on interest in the game of rugby (the greatest of team games).[7] Users of the coupon app SnipSnap are bonded together by their inclination to save money and share coupons with others. Likewise, the customer base of Bonobos.com is also an affiliate group, or an interest group formed around purchase behavior. Group members presumably also share tastes in value and fashion.

This last example gives us a nice way to think about how the virtual world organizes itself. If Bonobos had a store in, say, New Orleans, and that was *all* it had, then the "interest group" would most likely just consist of people who lived nearby (and perhaps tourists passing through the city as well). In short, the trading area of the seller — Bonobos — would be restricted to a rather small community of people sharing tastes, characteristics, *and* physical location.

One of the most fundamental things that the virtual world does is to allow the formation of groups and markets that don't (or can't) exist in the physical world. This raises interesting questions about how the virtual world is used and affects human behavior.

On the one hand, the Internet could lead to more diversity of interests. Everything from Spanish language courses to rugby debates to fashion advice to studies of obscure statistical methods is just a click away. You and I now have the opportunity to purse a diversity of interests as never before. We could embrace all kinds of new things.

On the other hand, for almost any kind of interest or activity, there is now also access to a sufficient density of others who are just a clique away (pun intended).

Researchers at Boston University and MIT looked at the issue of vicinity in the virtual world. They started with a simple but compelling premise: "Information technology can link geographically separated people and help them locate useful or interesting resources."[8] Then, using some abstract math, the authors determined that when people

---

7   Some of you might be familiar with the following quote attributed, in 1972, to the former rugby player Henry Blaha: "Rugby is a beastly game played by gentlemen; soccer is a gentleman's game played by beasts; football is a beastly game played by beasts."

8   Marshall Van Alstyne and Erik Brynjolfsson, "Global Village or Cyber-Balkans? Modeling and Measuring the Integration of Electronic Communities," *Management Science* 51, no. 6 (June 2005), 851–68.

unite around preferences—rather than around physical geography—
they may generate groups with very narrow interests.

So, what actually happens?

Do people become more diverse in their interests, or are they more
likely to focus on narrower cliques related to their preexisting interests?
The authors show, mathematically, that as access to others improves,
"agents" (or individual consumers) tend to seek out similar types of individuals in the virtual world and *give up some of their local connections
in the real world*. They conclude by noting that "preferences, not geography" may become the driving force in community formation and
delineation of community boundaries in the virtual world.

Take me, for example.

I am somewhat loath to admit this, but thanks to the wonders of the
virtual world, I've diverted at least part of my day from conversations
with friends and colleagues to reading rugby news on various sites including Rugby365.com and RugbyHeaven.com. My real-world preferences are driving me to affiliate with like-minded others in the virtual
world.

Expanding Distances and Shrinking Interests

So, we have the ability to become diverse in our affiliations or more narrow in terms of whom and what we associate with. On balance, and, as
indicated by my personal rugby example, balkanization appears to be
the stronger force and one nice piece of evidence comes from a study of
coauthorship patterns among academics.

Researchers in Canada found that before the widespread availability
of the Internet, academic coauthorships were quite diverse (I'll explain
what I mean by this in a moment), if somewhat constrained by geography.[9] They wanted to see whether things remained this way after the
introduction of the Internet. In particular, they were interested in how

---

9   Technically, the article looks at the effect of the adoption of Bitnet, an early version of the
    Internet. For more details, see Ajay Agrawal and Avi Goldfarb, "Restructuring Research:
    Communication Costs and the Democratization of University Innovation," *American Eco-
    nomic Review* 98, no. 4 (September 2008), 1578–90.

"changes in collaboration costs may affect the structure of knowledge production." Now *that* is certainly an eloquent way to state a research goal!

Prior to the advent of the Internet, it was relatively common for researchers in broadly related fields but with different focuses to team up and work on something interesting. This kind of diversity is usually seen as a good thing for the creation of overall knowledge.

Perhaps an econometrician from Penn, for example, and a labor economist from Georgetown (a little over one hundred miles away) would write papers together. The latter might provide the key ideas and theory, and the former would crunch the data and work out the empirical findings.

Enter the virtual world of the Internet.

Once the Internet came along, the average *geographic* distance between coauthors increased. The econometrician from Penn became more likely to team up with someone from farther away — perhaps a coauthor at the University of Zurich.

This is consistent with the theory I described earlier. Affiliations become more about taste and preferences and less about geography when the physical distance between people becomes less of an impediment to communication.

Even more interesting is the finding that coauthors are now more likely to align according to skills and interests versus proximity. The econometrician from Penn became more likely to work with another author with *more similar* skills; e.g., the colleague from Zurich is more likely to be an econometrician or statistician. (Perhaps someone just like my good friend the statistician Dr. Michael Wolf.[10])

Whether this is a good or bad thing is hard to say. But what *is* clear is that the "death of distance" has in some instances led to more narrowly circumscribed associations.

On the distinctively positive side, the researchers in Canada found that "multi-institutional collaboration" increased significantly post-Internet — by about 40 percent. In the language of economics, there were significant "gains from trade," with additional researchers (per-

---

10 Dr. Wolf's faculty page at the University of Zurich is at www.econ.uzh.ch/faculty/wolf.html.

haps from universities with underutilized research equipment) coming into proximity with collaborators who had access to a wider portfolio of resources.

Birds of a Virtual Feather

Members of virtual neighborhoods tend to be not only pretty cohesive in terms of dedication to an interest (if you haven't already done so, just take a look at the comments section in Rugby365.com) but also often quite geographically dispersed.

However, people who gather into virtual groups (whether to buy products or to discuss and create content) tend to share offline circumstances. Bonobos.com customers don't just share a common interest in fashionable clothing. More often than not, they share real-world circumstances too, in the sense that even though their physical locations are far apart, these customers live among similar kinds of neighbors, have similar access to offline stores, and so on. They may be starved of fashionable boutiques and therefore must look to the Internet for liberation.

As another example, take CitrusLane.com, a deliverer of "care packages to help moms and dads on their parenting journeys."[11] Citrus Lane's customers live all over the United States and consist mostly of people with young kids who also like the idea of having boxes of new products delivered to their home or office every month. So, they exhibit a key property of a virtual-world neighborhood: geographic separation combined with common or shared preferences.

More subtly, these customers, on average, have similar offline circumstances. CitrusLane.com offers products that are often hard to find or are otherwise hard to access locally in markets with relatively limited offline options. So its customers from Wisconsin (for example) are likely to have both preferences and offline options that are very similar to those of its customers from Texas.

---

11 This description comes from Citrus Lane's website, wwws.citruslane.com/about-us.

Packing In or Spreading Out

If you're a seller, then the "structure" of neighborhood formation in the virtual world matters a lot. Customers need to be accumulated carefully. Imagine that you've just completed a pilot for a new TV show and that you'd like to get people talking about it. Now, assume that you could somehow "seed," or start one hundred conversations about your show in order to try to get a bit of buzz humming along. Would you rather have ten different *groups* of people engaged in ten different chats about your show in ten different locations, or one single group of people discussing it intensively in one hundred different conversations?

If you picked the former (ten by ten) you have good instincts!

It turns out that if you want to generate awareness about what you're doing, it's generally better to have "width" rather than "depth," holding the total volume of word of mouth constant. Of course, you need some critical mass to begin with, but on average you are better off having things spread out over many locations. This idea was elaborated on and corroborated by researchers from Yale and Harvard who analyzed the short-term success of new TV shows.[12]

In the virtual world, as in the real one, "spread" or *dispersion* of information about your product, helps a lot. Of course, it almost always helps to have more information than less, but for a fixed amount of discourse about what you're up to, it's better to have it spread out rather than concentrated.

REAL-WORLD INFLUENCE ON VIRTUAL-WORLD NEIGHBORHOODS

Most of us participate in virtual-world communities of one sort or another — Facebook, LinkedIn, Twitter, Quora, SnapChat, Vine, etc. Our behavior in these places is of interest to social scientists, entrepreneurs,

---

12 David Godes and Dina Mayzlin, "Using Online Conversations to Study Word-of-Mouth Communications," *Marketing Science* 23, no. 4 (November 2004), 545–60.

sellers, advertisers, regulators, and even law enforcement.[13] As you might expect by now, participants' physical location and physical-world characteristics shape what goes on here too.

Sellers Advertising to Your Friends on Facebook

Pretend that you're an expert in social advertising and engaged in a consulting assignment for a large brand. For the sake of illustration, let's say that it's Coke (since Coke held the number one position in the Top 100 Global Brands for many years before being supplanted by Apple and was valued at nearly $80 billion in 2013 according to Interbrand).[14]

Now let's say that you can identify a set of users on Facebook who are "friends of Coke," and that one of these people is called Mary. These "friends of Coke" have an interest in soda and exhibit loyalty toward Coke in particular. Of course, in addition to being friends with the brand Coke, they'll no doubt have other (human) friends as well.

Now imagine that you advise Coke to send Facebook advertisements to either (a) random people on Facebook or (b) to *friends of people who are friends of Coke*. In other words, a subset of people like Mary's friends who satisfy the following condition: they are *not* friends of Coke themselves, but they are friends of people who *are* friends of Coke, in this case Mary.

Which group, (a) or (b), will deliver a higher response to the advertisements and why?

If you said the people belonging to group (b)—those who are *not* friends of Coke but *are* friends of Mary, who is a friend of Coke— you're right. A study conducted at MIT by Catherine Tucker found that Facebook advertising by a brand that is targeted at people who are

---

13 An interesting statistic for those concerned about privacy: according to the *Straits Times* of Singapore, in 2012 the US government made requests to Facebook for data on more than 21,000 users. See Derrick Ho, "Singapore Among World Governments That Requested Facebook Details About Users," *Straits Times*, August 28, 2013, www.straitstimes.com/breaking-news/singapore/story/singapore-among-world-governments-requested-facebook-details-about-use.

14 "Best Global Brands 2013," Interbrand, 2013, http://www.interbrand.com/en/best-global-brands/2013/Best-Global-Brands-2013.aspx.

"friends of people who are friends of that brand" has click-through rates that are *twice* those for ads sent to a random sample of people.[15]

The reason?

It comes back to one of our favorite terms, and our favorite real-world phenomenon, homophily.

If you are friends with Coke, and I am friends with you, then chances are that I have a higher inclination to consume sugary carbonated cola beverages than the average person does. Our friendship is an *indication* that we probably share tastes, interests, preferences, and perhaps (at least at one time) even physical locations as well.

So, friendship in the real world can, on average, be a reliable proxy for response to stimuli in the virtual one. This is an extremely powerful insight for sellers: physical-world relationships impact virtual-world responses to marketing and advertising.

The effects of homophily on virtual-world behavior are quite complex though, and it pays for sellers to be careful when they leverage it. For example, the MIT study shows that sellers should not to be too pushy with the ad copy. When Tucker changed the text of the advertising from benign appeals such as "be like your friend" to the more aggressive "your friend knows," the effectiveness of the advertising was greatly diminished (that is, click-through rates dropped).

Real-World Characteristics, Influence, and Signaling in the Virtual World

Researchers at UCLA looked at communities (or clusters of friends) in the virtual world and tried to understand who was influential for whom, what held the community together, and what, if anything, was the role of real-world characteristics.[16] After studying tens of thousands

---

15 Catherine Tucker, "Social Advertising" (working paper, Sloan School of Management, Massachusetts Institute of Technology, Cambridge, Massachusetts, 2012). In this study the "brand" is a charity for high school girls in East Africa. The click-through rate for friends of individuals who are "friends" of the charity on Facebook is much higher than for individuals who generally express an interest in education or charity.

16 Michael Trusov, Anand V. Bodapati, and Randolph E. Bucklin, "Determining Influential Users in Internet Social Networks," *Journal of Marketing Research* 47, no. 4 (August 2010), 643–58.

of users and their interactions, the authors arrived at three pretty fascinating conclusions.

First, they found that there is significant variation in the extent of influence that happens in virtual-world networks, both in the capacity of one individual to influence another in that network and in the susceptibility of an individual to fall under the influence of others.

Let's make this tangible with an example. Let's assume you and I both have one thousand friends on Facebook. That's a pretty decent number, especially when you compare it to the so-called Dunbar's number. Dunbar's number states that we can only maintain about 150 "proper" friendships in the real world. Anyway, continuing with the example, you and I have friendship networks that are exactly the same size.

The authors identified many cases in which two users (such as you and me) were operating in virtual-world neighborhoods that were basically identical in terms of size, but the "network impacts" (amount of total influence going on) varied by up to a factor of eight.

That's a lot! Perhaps in your network everyone is highly interconnected, influencing others and being subject to influence from them too. My network might, relatively speaking, be a network of "loners" who are much less engaged.

Second, we are each influenced, on average, by about 20 percent of our friends. Whether this is a big or small number is hard to say, but it feels about right doesn't it? One in five of your friends holds a bit of sway, or influence, over you. Of course you might be thinking "my Facebook network is really diverse, as my 'friends' are everyone from my best friend of the last ten years to someone I connected with last week." If that's true, then it's quite hard to detect and measure influence among "friends." The researchers recognized this issue too so by "influence" they mean that when one user in a virtual-world network starts doing something like posting or chatting, others follow and begin to initiate similar activity. On the flip side, about one third of the people in virtual communities are not influenced by anyone at all. They just do their own thing. Perhaps you can think of some of your Facebook friends who fit this description.

Third, and perhaps most interesting, the study found that patterns of influence in virtual-world social networks among users in the same vicinity, i.e., clusters of friends, are also driven and shaped by real-world factors.

For starters, your real-world gender matters a lot in terms of how much influence you have in the virtual world. If you're a woman then you're influential, on average, over the males in your social network. Conversely, male friends tend to exert weak influence over each other; female friends exert relatively weak influence over other females too. In fact, the only statistically significant effect found throughout all the clusters in the networks studied was females leading and males following.

Perhaps our two worlds, real and virtual, aren't that different after all!

Similarly, your ethnicity and age and your tenure in the network have important effects on your ability to be influential as well. The people in your virtual-world neighborhood who influence you the most have been in the vicinity longer (i.e., they have spent more months on the network), are younger than you, and have the same ethnicity as you.

These findings provide a nice segue to a study of dating behavior on Match.com, conducted by researchers at Duke and the University of Chicago.[17] After investigating the actual offline dating behavior of people who were paired up at the site Match.com, the researchers of the study observed systematic real-world/virtual-world patterns.

For example, people of both genders express very weak preferences for ethnicity. That is, most signal that they are willing to date others of any ethnic background. In reality, however, most *real-world dates* occur between partners of the same ethnicity. Perhaps there is some kind of "social signaling" going on here through which people like to convey the quality of openness across ethnic lines in order to secure dates, even when they ultimately tend to pair up with others of the same ethnicity.

Males tend to systematically overstate their income and women tend to systematically understate their weight.

(Please don't shoot me. I'm just the messenger.)

So there are systematic discrepancies between what people *say* they are and will do in the virtual world, and what they *actually* are and are willing to do in the real world. If you find this all rather amusing,

---

17 Günter Hitsch, Ali Hortaçsu, and Dan Ariely, "What Makes You Click? — Mate Preferences in Online Dating" (working paper, University of Chicago, Chicago, Illinois, 2010).

then there are plenty of other fun things to be discovered just by typing "most stupid profile on Match.com" into your search engine.[18]

It also turns out that just revealing your real-world dating status in a virtual-world network makes you *less* influential. The researchers from UCLA found that users on social networking sites who indicate that they are "looking for a date" have significantly *less* influence over others in their vicinity (their virtual neighborhood), than the average person does. In fact, this effect was the largest statistically significant effect of all—almost twice as large as the second-biggest effect: the number of months a user has been part of the network.

So, if you joined a social networking site early, you're more influential on it, but if you're prowling around looking for dates, you're far less so. (And if that's what you're up to, then it might make sense to keep it to yourself.)

Vicinity and Demand at Virtual-World Sellers

It's now time to pull all of these ideas together in one integrative example.

I concluded chapter 3 (ADJACENCY) by showing how the sales at an Internet retailer spread over time and space and allowed the seller to amass customers from almost twenty thousand zip codes within a few short years. There, my emphasis was on adjacency and the idea that word about the company spread through real-world proximity.

Now I want to extend that idea by showing—with the same dataset (for ease of comparison)—the powerful concept of vicinity in action. As we've seen in this chapter, the ties that bind are more than simply geographic. To get started on understanding the practical implications of this key idea, imagine that you reside in a zip code in Los Angeles, California. Then also imagine that there is an "identical" zip code elsewhere in the country.

If this is true (and it is), then your location and its doppelganger might both contain customers with the same level of interest in retail-

---

18 Here's one result: http://scholarsandrogues.com/2013/01/08/meet-the-men-of-match-com-really-guys-are-you-serious/.

ers like Netgrocer.com. Or Amazon. Or Bonobos.com, Harrys.com, WarbyParker.com, or any number of other websites and apps as well, including those like Waze.com and Yelp.com that provide content rather than physical products.

HOMOPHILY, REVISITED

Geographic Neighbors and Demographic Doppelgangers[19]

My coauthors and I wanted to test the idea that an Internet seller develops its customer base in clusters, first through proximity and later through what we termed "demographic similarity." To do so, we examined the diffusion of Netgrocer.com throughout the state of Pennsylvania. At the time we were all living in Philadelphia, so we thought, why not just start with the Keystone State?

For each of the more than fifteen hundred zip codes in Pennsylvania, we defined the immediate zip code neighbors using the approach discussed in the previous chapter. That is, we determined that 19103 is bordered by 19102, 19104, and so on. Just as we did in the analysis of the effect of adjacency, every zip code was then identified in terms of its *geographic neighbors.*

Next we used data from the US Census to describe all of those more than fifteen hundred zip codes in terms of the *characteristics* of the residents who lived in them. We focused on age, income, education, and ethnicity as the core variables. We then formed all possible pairs of zip codes from the over fifteen hundred that we were analyzing.[20]

Then, for each pair, we computed their *demographic* similarity. By that I mean we would figure out how "close" two zip codes are in terms of the makeup of the residents who live there.

In total, we used fifteen different characteristics—things like "percentage of residents with university degrees" and "percentage of resi-

---

19 If you're like more than 130,000 others (as of August 2013) and you want to find your celebrity doppelganger, then head to www.findmydoppelganger.com and search away!

20 This is a pretty big number, since the total of all possible pairs is the so-called triangular number $n \times (n - 1) \div 2$ where n is greater than 1,500 in this case. Thank goodness for computers!

dents with income over $75,000 per year"—and tested different mathematical approaches to computing what we termed demographic similarity.[21]

Armed with this information, we set about to explain and predict how many new customers would appear in each zip code in Pennsylvania each month after Netgrocer.com opened their site.

Long-Distance Homophily

The concept behind this is something that I've stressed throughout the book. If two real-world locations tend to be similar in terms of the residents who live in them, then, everything else being equal, those locations might have similar levels of demand for a virtual-world business, whether that business is selling products or content.

So, while Philadelphia is closer to Harrisburg (about seventy miles away) than it is to Pittsburgh (about three hundred miles away), the individuals who live in Philadelphia are more likely to have tastes and traits in common with people in Pittsburgh than with those in Harrisburg. These commonalities of traits and tastes will show up as similar patterns of demand for a specific virtual-world seller.

This observation is a direct application of the concepts put forth by the sociologist Claude Fischer that I discussed at the beginning of the chapter—i.e., that Angelenos and Chicagoans have more in common and more contact with one another than Chicagoans and residents of Springfield, Illinois, do.

In addition, it's likely that a "clone" of my Philadelphia residential zip code, PA 19123, exists not only elsewhere within Pennsylvania but also elsewhere within the United States as well. In fact, its demographic profile (e.g., the age, income, education, and ethnicity) can help us identify "neighbors" near and far.

So "closeness" is defined in terms of physical proximity, and it can be defined in terms demographic similarity as well. We can often find two

---

21 If you're interested in the details, please see the Web Appendix E at http://www.marketing power.com/jmrfeb10 that accompanies the article by Jeonghye Choi, Sam K. Hui, and David R. Bell, "Spatiotemporal Analysis of Imitation Behavior Across New Buyers at an Online Grocery Retailer," *Journal of Marketing Research* 47, no. 1 (February 2010), 75–89.

(or more) locations that are far apart in terms of *physical* closeness but actually very close together in terms of the *similarity of their residents*.

A DEEPER LOOK AT SALES EVOLUTION FOR
AN INTERNET SELLER

Proximity and More

At the end of chapter 3 (ADJACENCY), I brought the ideas concerning real-world proximity, adjacency, and contagion to life in one example that showed how they all played out together. There, the closeness of two neighborhoods (zip codes) was defined according to physical location only. I showed that consumers' demand spread rapidly over time through contiguity, from one proximate zip code to the next.

Now, armed with the additional insights I've developed in this chapter about vicinity, we can return to the same sales process and look at it a little more carefully.[22]

In going back to what we knew about adjacency and contagion, and trying to get a deeper understanding of the pattern underlying how new customers are acquired by Internet sellers, my coauthors and I focused on three key factors: (1) the number of existing customers *within* a zip code, (2) the number of existing customers across all the zip code's *geographic* neighbors, and (3) the number of customers across the zip code's *demographic* neighbors.

What we found was quite striking, and I've since had the opportunity to see the pattern repeat for many other Internet sellers as well.

First, there is a very strong immediate neighbor effect.

The greater the number of existing customers that are already present in a real-world zip code, the greater the number of new virtual-world customers who tend to show up in subsequent months. This is just the micro-level manifestation of everything we've discussed in terms of adjacency: people in close physical proximity have a tendency

---

22 Academic research often proceeds this way. You examine a theory and data and gain some insight into a new phenomenon. In arriving at the new insight, you realize that even more digging is warranted, so you go back to uncover the next layer of finding. This is the essence of programmatic research.

to talk to each other, observe each other, and therefore sometimes to imitate each other as well.

Second, we found that sales took off initially in what we came to term "hot spots" and spread out from there. In Pennsylvania these hot spots were the major cities in the state, Philadelphia and Pittsburgh. Over time, however, the rate of growth of new customers in these hot spots and their surrounding zip codes started to slow down. Or, if you like, the early real-world locations eventually became "tapped out" in terms of their ability to keep generating new customers and virtual-world sales.

So, what about zip codes elsewhere in the state that were very similar in terms of the characteristics of their residents, yet were perhaps hundreds of miles apart?

We found that zip codes in the same vicinity (in terms of their demographic characteristics, *not* proximity), started to generate new customers at similar times and at about the same rate.

Thus, new customers for this virtual-world seller were being generated by two important things: short-range proximity (within and across zip codes) and comparable zip codes that were considerable distances from each other.

There was another unexpected component to the story too, specifically the even more striking way that the strength of the effects unfolded over time for the seller.

In the first couple of years, most new customers were generated by the geographic proximity effect. As time wore on, however, more and more customers were acquired in locations that were distant from each other but very similar in their demographic profile. In fact, absent the ability of the seller to get this *second-order* dynamic going—i.e., tap demand through demographic similarity—the business might well have collapsed.

The Spatial Long Tail

We're over halfway on our journey together through this book, so now might be an appropriate time for me to introduce some important new jargon (hinted at in the introduction). It's a semioriginal concept: the *Spatial Long Tail* (SLT).[23]

Where does this term come from?

Well, when we plotted the number of new customers in a histogram against the real-world locations that generated them, we uncovered an intriguing phenomenon. In the SLT the x-axis shows all the counties in the state of Pennsylvania, ranked from those with the most customers to those with the least (going from left to right, so that the resulting graph slopes downward). The y-axis just shows the number of customers in each county.

When we computed this histogram and drew it up we noticed a pattern very similar to that described by Chris Anderson in his book *The Long Tail*.[24]

If you've read the book, please bear with me for a moment. If not, I highly recommend that you read it cover to cover (what follows here is just the CliffsNotes, or shorthand, version of the part relevant for this discussion).

The core idea in Chris Anderson's book is very powerful.

It starts with an observation about product supply and availability, namely, that the Internet has dramatically reduced the costs of offering variety — Amazon can carry millions of books whereas even a very large physical store would struggle to carry more than, say, 100,000.

If you were running Amazon and selling millions of books, you could attempt the following: At the end of the year, you could total the sales for each book and rank the books from best- to worst-selling. If you did, you'd notice a pattern.

You'd have a few books that sold really well — books like Harry Potter and the Bible. You'd also have hundreds of thousands of books that sold hardly at all, perhaps just one or two copies. If you drew a histogram of product sales, starting from the most popular product all the way down

---

23 Like a BLT — but more interesting and less delicious!

24 Besides having a great title, *The Long Tail: Why the Future of Business Is Selling Less of More* (New York: Hyperion, 2006), the book has a lot of provocative and interesting ideas. I can't do them all justice here, but I'll elaborate on the main idea because the implications it has for sales of different types of *products* (mainstream and niche) has a direct parallel to sales from different types of *locations* (mainstream and niche).

to the least popular product, you'd see that the *total* sales from all those rather slow sellers would actually add up to a pretty significant number.

Specifically, if you drew a vertical line in the histogram with all the books with sales ranks of, say, 1 to 100,000 to the left of the line and those ranked 100,001 and higher to the right, you'd observe that books to the right of the line, i.e., those in the "tail," might account for up to a quarter of all your profits!

The "head" of the diagram is the popular stuff (the books that would actually make it onto a physical bookstore shelf), and the "tail" is the niche or relatively unpopular stuff.

And so it is with location.

Netgrocer.com certainly needed to make the sales to customers in Philadelphia and Allegheny counties (the first two counties in the "head," with the most sales), but they needed far more than that as well. Without the customers in the "tail" locations, they would not have survived. Those long-tail locations contribute a lot to a virtual-world seller's bottom line.[25]

Here's another interesting thing about head vs. tail locations.

Customers in the head locations were acquired largely via proximity effects. Adjacency among physical locations facilitated the spreading of word of mouth and emulation as well. Customers in the tail locations, on the other hand, were generated via similarity.

This is because there is an 80/20 weighting at the beginning of the virtual-world sales process, in which 80 percent of the new customers initially came from proximity effects, which eventually gave way to a 50/50 balance once the business stabilized.

So while physical adjacency of locations is critical in explaining how the real world drives the virtual world, a deeper dig reveals that vicinity and the broader definition of a cluster or neighborhood that I've used here plays a vital role as well.

To make sure that this evolution by proximity first and similarity second was actually a robust pattern, we put our model to the test. We pretended that we could "seed" locations with some number of new

---

25 If you like analogies, then think back to our discussions of gravity; for a traditional retail store, there really isn't much of a "tail" to speak of at all. The trading area is limited to just the immediate zip codes around the store, so any "long-tail" plot would just have a head, which declines rapidly, followed by a lot of zeros.

customers, and then we saw how different approaches to seeding would have different effects on the overall sales evolution.

That is, we ran a lot of simulations on our computers.

So, let's imagine that we could magically go out and drop new customers into fifty locations that didn't have customers just yet.

How should we choose those locations so as to maximize the seller's overall growth? Should we put a new customer into each of the fifty most populous regions? Spread them around randomly? Drop them in the locations with the fewest number of customers to date?

Well, it turns out that each of these approaches has pros and cons.

As you might imagine, dropping new customers into locations that are underperforming (relative to their population size) does pretty well—at least for a while.

But the *best* approach is to focus initially on relatively well-populated areas and thereby take advantage of the proximity effect. Then, as the rate of new-customer growth stabilizes, online sellers should then alter their strategies to pick up new customers via the similarity effect.

When we used this combined approach, we saw vastly superior results. Our findings reveal that most Internet sellers should start in well-populated locations but then seek footholds in other places as well, places that are all grouped in the same vicinity through the shared real-world characteristics, circumstances, and sets of preferences held by the residents there.

The overall message is that spatially dispersed customer seeding is generally superior to seeding that is spatially clustered.[26] Sean Rad and Justin Mateen, founders of the wildly successful hookup and dating app Tinder, implicitly recognized this principle when they seeded Southern Methodist University in Dallas, Texas, immediately after getting traction at the University of Southern California, in Los Angeles.[27]

Again, this is something that I've seen over and over. It's Chris Anderson's Long Tail idea in action once again, but this time with a spatial twist—the SLT.

---

26 Other researchers have reported complementary results. See, for example, Barak Libai, Eitan Muller, and Renna Peres, "The Role of Seeding in Multi-Market Entry," *International Journal of Research in Marketing* 22, no. 4 (December 2005), 375–93.

27 http://www.gq.com/life/relationships/201402/tinder-online-dating-sex-app?currentPage=2.

Summary

There's the neighborhood that you dwell in, but there are others you reside in and "live" in as well. Ones based not on proximity, but rather on culture, demographics, buying behavior, and preferences. Coalesced around interests, birds of a virtual feather, are joined together. Defined less by proximity and more by preferences, these new groupings can be quite narrowly construed. Followers of rugby (Rugby365.com), fans of "peacock" pants (Bonobos.com), and academic collaborators separated by greater distances but joined by narrower ideas. Given the opportunity, you might end up "linking" only to others who are just like you!

Virtual-world influence comes in a variety of real-world flavors too. If you want to have sway over others, it helps to be younger, female, and an early member of the virtual-world community. Perhaps less surprisingly, some virtual-world types like to obscure their real-world identities and fudge things a little. (Men like to overstate their real-world height and incomes.)

Within every country, there are "doppelganger" locations all over the place. Since the trading areas of virtual-world sellers are very large, it should be possible to attract customers from these "sister" locations. Building on chapter 3 (ADJACENCY) we saw that Internet sellers benefit first from initial sales to customers in close *physical proximity*. Then, if they're fortunate, they later expand their trading area to more distant doppelganger locations, where they get subsequent sales arising from the *demographic similarity* among distant but comparable neighborhoods.

The end result is the Spatial Long Tail, in which the *head* is demand from customers connected through "proximity," and the *tail* is demand from customers connected by "similarity." A large pool of customers still comes from the "main" locations, but all the smaller locations matter too, and collectively add up to a lot!

Value comes from vicinity — you'll succeed when you collect head and tail locations together.

Five

ISOLATION

Why Isolation Offline Means Liberation Online: How the Virtual World Empowers "Preference Minorities"

I•SO•LA•TION *n.*
The act of isolating, the quality or condition of being isolated.

In chapter 3 (ADJACENCY) and chapter 4 (VICINITY), I explained why things spread via contiguity and how online neighborhoods form without regard to physical distance, respectively. Geographic clustering happens naturally and is a powerful driver of information sharing and emulation. Demographic clustering is a more subtle kind of association—groups that form around shared characteristics and shared preferences end up in the same market vicinity.

In this chapter I explore the final and most "micro" piece of the puzzle in the A-V-I sequence at the center of our GRAVITY framework.

I focus on the inherent motivation that we all have to liberate ourselves from our real-world circumstances because of *whom* we have chosen to live among.

This might seem a little paradoxical, because at the beginning of the book I explained how where we choose to live is based, in part, on cost-benefit trade-offs concerning the goods and services that a location offers.

That is, of course, still correct!

Homophily, a key part of this fact and an important principle for our analysis, also dictates that people who have made similar trade-offs and ended up in the same location will, on average, share characteristics.

Now, all of this notwithstanding, there can still be many instances in which we *do* differ from our neighbors in meaningful ways. Perhaps you have a newborn yet most of your neighbors are older, with children in high school or grown up and out of the house.

Alternatively, perhaps you came from some other country (say, New Zealand) and you have tastes and preferences for products and services (vegemite and international rugby matches) that are not too popular among others in your location.

In this chapter, I now look at what it means to suffer from this special form of isolation, called preference isolation, and how the virtual world can liberate you from it. I'll take us through the key nuances of preference isolation, elaborate the general concept, and then conclude with a more detailed analysis of one of my own research studies, which shows the principle in action.

Drivers and Elements of Preference Isolation

Take a look around your local neighborhood.

Or just reflect on it for a moment. What kinds of goods and services are offered there? Are you happy with the selection of bars and restaurants, the variety of products in the supermarket, the distance that you have to travel to get to the dry cleaners, and so on?

As we saw in chapter 1 (GEOGRAPHY), central place theory tells us that the overall amount of stuff available to you will be dictated by the size of the market that you live in. The bigger the place, the more goods and services it offers. Now, since you're a rational person, you've selected where to live, in part, on the basis of what is offered in that location.

So far, so good.

But in this chapter I am going to explore the very important idea that you just might want to get things that aren't readily available to you locally. Here's why. Like you, the managers running the local businesses in your neighborhood are also pretty rational. They face constraints—such as the size of their trading area, the preferences of those who live in it, and the physical size of their establishments—and decide what to offer accordingly. So, whether or not they pay attention to what *you* want depends on how much overlap your wants have with those of others in your neighborhood.

Now, there are two kinds of real-world isolation that are important drivers of how we use the virtual world. We discussed the first one, *geographic* isolation, quite extensively in chapter 2, RESISTANCE. If you live a long way from real-world stores, none of them has much hold over you. Their gravitational pull is weak, so you're attracted to the Internet. In general, the amount of "pull" a commercial establishment like a store or restaurant has over you is a function of how close it is and how "good" it is—in terms of offering you what you want. It's hard to stay out of a place that's right next to you and has everything you need, and at great prices to boot.

Earlier we saw examples of how this works in both directions. An increase in the distance you need to travel to an offline store makes the Internet more attractive. When new offline stores open up in your neighborhood, the Internet becomes less attractive.

The second condition—*preference* isolation—is more subtle but just as powerful. Let's introduce it through an example.

Consider that retail stores (and bars, restaurants, and other establishments as well) try to stock products that: (1) their customers like, and (2) provide the highest possible profit-to-merchandizing-effort ratio. Merchandizing effort includes things such as the amount of shelf space needed, the marketing budget, and so on.

What this means in practical terms is that sellers in a particular location will tend to cater to the tastes of the majority. If retailers, for example, don't have much room to stock soda, then Coke and Pepsi will get most of the space (perhaps even to the complete exclusion of Dr. Pepper). If you want Diet Dr. Pepper with lime, but no one else in your neighborhood does, you might be tough out of luck.

Preferences and the Radio Star

Before examining how isolation drives us into the virtual world, it helps to first understand the relationship between the size of the available market and the extent of the product variety offered there.

To demonstrate the relationship, a colleague at the University of Pennsylvania undertook a comprehensive study of the US radio market and determined that larger (real-world) markets had both more stations and a population that spent a greater amount of time listening to radio.[1] This is a case of a "positive externality" from others in the sense that the more people there are in your real-world location, the more variety of media there will be for you to consume.

However, in many instances, specific individuals not only have strong preferences for *particular versions* of a product, but also tend to *not like* versions of the product that have been targeted at *other* consumers. In radio, this phenomenon is especially stark.

Data used in the study, supplied the market research agency Arbitron, show just how polarized preferences for different formats of radio actually are. While some kinds of formats, for example, "soft rock," are programmed for generic or mass appeal, others clearly cater to audiences along ethnic lines. Listening data from these stations show very pronounced patterns.

Throughout the United States, more than 96 percent of those listening to the so-called narrowly targeted Hispanic-focused radio format are Hispanic. (Non-Hispanic listeners are less than one half of one percent of the audience!). Similarly, for black-focused radio, between 82 and 92 percent of the listening audience is black.[2]

The subtleties of what gets offered in these real-world markets provide a nice foundation for understanding what happens when the virtual world comes into play to liberate those who have unmet needs. First, more people bring forth more stations (i.e., larger markets just have more variety). In many ways this is just another manifestation of central place theory as discussed in chapter 1 (GEOGRAPHY). And this

---

1   Joel Waldfogel, "Preference Externalities: An Empirical Study of Who Benefits Whom in Differentiated-Product Markets," *RAND Journal of Economics* 34, no. 3 (Autumn 2003), 557–68.

2   The precise number depends on the sub-format, e.g., "black/adult contemporary" (85 percent), "black/gospel" (94 percent).

effect is especially strong *within* a particular ethnicity and type of station, so a larger sized market does *not* benefit everyone equally. Adding more whites to the overall population has the effect of bringing forth more stations, but only more stations targeted to whites will emerge (the effect of more whites in the overall population on stations targeted to blacks is negligible). Likewise, adding more blacks to the total population helps to bring forth more black-targeted stations but has practically zero effect on the number of stations targeting whites.

So, adding certain "types" to a market creates more variety for those types, but not necessarily for others.

Reading (and Writing) the Newspaper

In a study related to the radio study, researchers at the University of Chicago and the University of Pennsylvania examined the same kinds of ideas, but for newspapers.[3] The authors looked at more than 250 markets throughout the United States and again found evidence of strong preference externalities.

Blacks were much more likely to purchase newspapers, in general, in markets that contained a majority of blacks, but were actually less likely to buy them in markets that contained more whites (everything else held constant). Newspapers, like radio stations, tend to produce content targeted at least partially along ethnic lines.

Hence, a black person living in a predominantly white town might not be able to access news of interest locally.

The radio and newspaper studies illustrate two important points. First, the preference minority status of certain individuals could be indicated by characteristics that are easily observed and tabulated (e.g., in the census and other places). So far I have been focusing on examples to do with ethnicity. However, not all observable characteristics of individuals are equally helpful.

Take gender, for example.

The male-female split doesn't vary that much across cities and towns

3 Lisa George and Joel Waldfogel, "Who Affects Whom in Daily Newspaper Markets?," *Journal of Political Economy* 111, no. 4 (August 2003), 765–84.

in the United States (and most other places). So it's probably going to be hard to find any males or females that are isolated in their gender-specific preferences—i.e., living in real-world markets that don't really cater to them at all. Hence, characteristics that vary *a lot* by geography are much more useful than gender for determining preference minority status.

Second, preference minority status could be attributable to having a characteristic that is temporary, such as being the parent of a newborn child. This is the example that I mentioned at the beginning of the chapter, and I'll discuss it in more detail later on. The fraction of households with children in a market, and therefore the number of people looking for diapers, formula, baby toys, and related products, does vary quite a bit across markets.

Now back to the news.

As well as consuming the news, it turns out that some of us are "producing it," loosely speaking, as well. Most newspapers and other media accept user-generated content (UGC) into their online editions. According to some reports, over half of the US population on the Internet—some 115 million people—contribute content to the Internet. For some time now, newspapers and other publications have lived both in the real world (for example, the *New York Times* print edition) and in the virtual world as well (www.nytimes.com).

Researchers in Pittsburgh and Philadelphia conducted a fascinating study of what the production of UGC does to the real- and virtual-world editions of the same newspaper.[4] The authors found that when you and I can contribute to an online newspaper, there's a surprising effect on the real-world version. The print versions of the papers become more mild in terms of the opinions expressed (particularly those of a political bent), while conversely, the online versions of the papers become more slanted, either to the left or to the right.

The virtual-world slanting is of course more extreme when generated from real-world locations that are strongly linked to one type of political viewpoint. That is, the commentary that gets added to the *New York Times* online version might be expected to be more left-leaning if it originates from a reader in San Francisco.

---

4   Pinar Yildirim, Esther Gal-Or, and Tansev Geylani, "User-Generated Content and Bias in News Media," *Management Science* 59, no. 12 (December 2013), 2655–66.

One final observation is worth making here.

Media markets (both real and virtual) are also important for civic engagement. Without access to news and content, individuals are less likely to participate in local affairs and, in particular, to vote in local and national elections, as it is more difficult to stay informed.

A study by researchers at Harvard and Penn looked at the relationship between the provision of real and virtual media and voting behavior.[5] In locations where there was a critical mass of Spanish-language residents, the local market provided real and virtual world news in Spanish. The presence of this media, in turn, had a very important effect on voter turnout—increasing it by as much as four percentage points over and above what it would have been absent a dedicated Spanish-language media channel.

Social Pressure and Preference Visibility

Another study, conducted by researchers at the University of Southern California and in Hong Kong, looked at the explicit manipulation of preference isolation in virtual-world networks.[6] They examined users' behavior on the leading social networking site in China, Kaixin001.com (roughly translated as "Happy Net"). Looking at virtual-world relationships among real-world friends, the authors asked, "When a person is surrounded by her friends, and only her friends, does she conform to or diverge from the most popular choice among them?"

The field experiment was conducted in a part of the site where users were employing an app called "Virtual Homes" to color and decorate virtual houses that they had built on the site. Over sixteen thousand users were subjected to an experiment in which they were told about the choices of others.

The focus was the color chosen by *other* users of the site.

---

5 Felix Oberholzer-Gee and Joel Waldfogel, "Media Markets and Localism: Does Local News en Español Boost Hispanic Voter Turnout?," *American Economic Review* 99, no. 5 (December 2009), 2120–28.

6 Monic Sun, Xiaoquan Zhang, and Feng Zhu, "To Belong or Be Different? Evidence from a Large-Scale Field Experiment in China" (working paper, Marshall School of Business, University of Southern California, Los Angeles, California, 2013).

In one condition, the subjects were told about the popularity of the color chosen by *all* users at the site. In the other condition, they were told about the popularity of the color chosen by *their friends*.

Interestingly, the popularity of the color selected by random users on the site had essentially no influence at all on what color the subjects chose to decorate their own virtual houses. Conversely, when informed that a *higher* percentage of their friends had chosen a particular color than any other (say, yellow) they became *less* likely to choose that color for themselves.

Finally, users in a third condition were told about the choices of their friends, but with one additional twist: they were also told that their own choice would be announced to their friends on the site.

Would this "social sharing" make a difference to the way the users presented themselves in the virtual world?

It turns out that the answer is yes.

Subjects were told that a particular color, say, yellow, was popular among their friends. The researchers manipulated the level of popularity from 50 to 60 percent and even up to 80 and 90 percent. They found that when the popularity of a color came close to unanimity, the subjects, who knew that they would have to announce their choice, became more likely to adopt it as well.

So, we have two different and very interesting forces of real-world friendship on virtual-world behavior. (Recall that the study was a comparison of the effect of actions taken by one's friends versus actions taken by random others in the network.) When portraying ourselves in the virtual world, we seem to like to diverge from what others do and retain a sense of individual expression—except when our choices will be publically announced *and* our friends are all doing the same thing.

It's nice to express your individuality unless you really have to swim against the tide of your friends in a very public way!

Isolation and Connecting to the Virtual World

Colleagues of mine conducted a clever evaluation of the relationship between Internet use and ethnicity in order to confirm that people who differ from their neighbors are more likely to be active in the virtual world. In particular, they examined whether the ethnicity of one's neighbors affects the Internet use of a particular individual.[7]

So in this instance, we're not just considering whether the lack of offline options *in general* drives people online (we know that it does), but taking the argument a step further. The question now is whether the absence of satisfying offline options for *specific individuals* who have minority preferences drives them online.

Recall also that in chapter 2 (RESISTANCE) we saw that the Internet can act as a substitute for cities by liberating people who live in smaller towns from their lack of product variety. But the finding we're discussing here is a bit stronger. It's not just the size of our city that matters for connectivity, but also how similar we are to those around us in terms of characteristics that are correlated with preferences, and the nature of those preferences themselves.

Real-World Benefits from Virtual-World Anonymity

On July 5, 1993, Peter Steiner published an iconic cartoon in the *New Yorker* that found its way to Internet lore. Perhaps you can recall seeing it. A dog perched on a chair in front of a desktop computer is saying to another pooch at his feet, "On the Internet, nobody knows you're a dog."

And so a simple cartoon epitomized the popular notion of the virtual world as a place for anonymity.

How might this anonymity impact real-world outcomes for individuals who might otherwise face discrimination and other pernicious effects?

Researchers at Berkeley, Yale, and J. D. Power (a market research company) looked at this in detail in one of the most important consumer markets in the United States (and in most economies for that

---

7   Todd Sinai and Joel Waldfogel, "Geography and the Internet: Is the Internet a Substitute or Complement for Cities?," *Journal of Urban Economics* 56, no. 1 (July 2004), 1–24.

matter), the automobile market.[8] They examined the prices paid by consumers across thousands of transactions and in numerous local markets throughout the country.

Sure enough, they found what other economists have documented many times in the past: members of minority populations tend to pay quite a bit more for their cars. To be clear, the researchers looked at the prices paid for *exactly the same* car by people of different ethnic backgrounds.

The data were definitive.

Black and Hispanic consumers paid about 2 percent more than other consumers did for the same car. (This percentage adds up to quite a few hundred dollars per person in this market, given that the price paid for a typical automobile is in the tens of thousands of dollars!)

About two thirds of that price premium (or about 1.4 percent of the extra amount these consumers were paying) can be explained by characteristics including consumers' income and education levels. That is, the entire 2 percent was not "pure" discrimination in the sense of it all being attributable to racial bias on the part of the car dealers. Now of course, education levels and income are sometimes correlated with ethnicity as well, but the authors adjusted for these correlations in the study.

What of the remaining one-third premium? Well, sadly, that is almost inevitably the result of racial discrimination.

Enter the virtual world of the Internet.

When shoppers performed several steps of the transaction (qualification, search, and so on) over the Internet, then the racial bias penalty disappeared completely! That is, since one can choose to be anonymous on the Internet, dealers were not able to figure out ethnicity or other cues like gender that typically enter the calculus of discrimination.

When an auto dealer gets a lead from "Dakota Smith," he or she will find it hard to say too much about what this person might look like. (According to one list, "Dakota" is the number one "gender neutral"

---

8   Florian Zettelmeyer, Fiona Scott Morton, and Jorge Silva-Risso, "Consumer Information and Discrimination: Does the Internet Affect the Pricing of New Cars to Women and Minorities?," *Quantitative Marketing and Economics* 1, no. 1 (March 2003), 65–92.

name for US babies in the sense that it's the most balanced of all names given to boys and girls.[9]) In some instances the virtual world is the perfect camouflage for those who can be disadvantaged or discriminated against in the real world.

Niche Products and Preference Isolation

Researchers at MIT compared Internet demand for apparel in locations with no nearby offline stores with demand in locations that had the median number of apparel stores. Demand in locations with the median number of stores was 4.2 percent *lower* than it was in locations with no stores.[10]

This suggests an interesting "balancing out" between the real and virtual worlds, in the sense that one makes up for the other. In locations where individuals were underserved by their local markets—online sales were higher. In locations where they were less isolated, in the sense of having greater access to offline apparel, online sales were significantly lower.

The researchers also discovered something that dovetailed with a finding that I presented and discussed in chapter 2 (RESISTANCE). There I noted that when physical bookstores open up in a neighborhood, sales at Amazon.com suffer—but only for popular books and not for obscure ones. The MIT researchers found something similar for apparel, concluding that

> Internet retailers face significant competition from brick-and-mortar retailers when selling mainstream products, but are virtually immune from competition when selling niche products.[11]

---

9 If you're interested in seeing other names then be sure to check out http://www.babynames1000.com/gender-neutral/.

10 See Erik Brynjolfsson, Jeffrey Hu, and Mohammed S. Rahman, "Battle of the Retail Channels: How Product Selection and Geography Drive Cross-Channel Competition," *Management Science* 55, no. 11 (November 2009), 1755–65.

11 Brynjolfsson, Hu, and Rahman, "Battle of the Retail Channels," 1755.

This finding is mostly explained by geographic isolation of customers and search frictions—the two key ideas in chapter 2 (RESISTANCE). Geographic distance and search friction make it relatively tough for consumers to track down niche items at offline stores. It takes too much time and effort, and for some items it may not even be possible at all. However, preference isolation of local customers plays an important role in explaining this finding as well. Niche products are bought by those with minority tastes, so virtual-world sellers can cater to these individuals without fear of competing head on with offline stores.

Researchers at MIT wanted to understand what would happen when retailers in the real and virtual worlds offered *identical* product assortments and prices. Would they have *identical* patterns of sales? In particular, they were interested to see if there would be differences in sales of products from the Long Tail—those desired by customers with more niche or isolated preferences.[12]

So, it's real-world (catalog) versus virtual-world (website).

The researchers found that even though the seller's offerings were identical in the two channels, the virtual-world channel of the Internet saw higher levels of sales for products located in the "tail" of the long-tail plot.[13]

Unit sales of niche products were 14.8 percent in the Internet channel, and dollar sales were 15.0 percent, compared with only 12.7 percent for both metrics in the catalog channel. The effects were highly statistically significant.

Since prices and assortments were identical, what could explain this discrepancy?

The big difference between the two channels is that shoppers with niche preferences were more able to *find* products in the "tail" on the Internet. This is because the virtual world of the Internet comes replete with recommendations from customers and with the ability to search. Regardless of their station in the real world, shoppers in the virtual world are more able to get into the tail and discover niche items.

---

12 Erik Brynjolfsson, Jeffrey Hu, and Duncan Simester, "Goodbye Pareto Principle, Hello Long Tail: The Effect of Search Cost on the Concentration of Product Sales," *Management Science* 57, no. 8 (August 2011), 1373–86.

13 For a refresher on the concept, please go back to chapter 4.

Preference Isolation in Action

I concluded chapters 3 (ADJACENCY) and 4 (VICINITY) by going into some detail on how the key ideas there came to life through my own research, and I'll do the same thing here.

This time I'll focus on research that I conducted using data from that intrepid supplier of all things baby related, Diapers.com. The concepts I describe here are equally relevant to other product categories, as long as local target customers are outnumbered by others with different preferences and therefore overlooked by local sellers.

BABY PRODUCTS AND VEGEMITE IN PHILADELPHIA

Prior to digging into a "proper" research exercise on preference isolation to really test it out (by "proper" I mean one that involved a lot of data and number crunching), my friend and collaborator Jeonghye and I decided to visit a few stores in the Philadelphia area and check out a fairly simple idea (more details in a moment).

But before embarking on this little field study, we realized that in order to get a full study done, we would need to be able to figure out two things.

First, for every location (zip code) in the United States, we had to know how urgent or common the need for baby-related products was. Again, in line with what I said at the beginning of the chapter, the "isolation" for customers in this example comes from a particular life state: the presence of newborns in the household.

Knowing the percentage of households with newborns in a zip code, i.e., the fraction of households with children, relative to the total number households in that zip code, would allow us to figure out whether an individual household in each location would, on average, be well served by the real world or not.

Of course, we could also look at isolation that might be correlated with other observable characteristics such as ethnicity, income, gender, or education level, but the point I want to put forth in this chapter about *preference isolation* is made more generally by focusing on markets for particular products and services, as we do here.

In this example, it's pretty easy to identify the customers of interest — it's people with young kids. Fortunately, the US government, via the US Census, provides detailed statistics on the presence of kids for every zip code in the country.

Also in this instance, products required by households with newborns are widely available in supermarkets, drugstores, and so on. That means we could also count the number of stores in each zip code — again, courtesy of data collected by the US government and other third-party commercial suppliers such as ESRI.[14]

Second, we would need an Internet business to share its sales data with us. That way we could compare the urgency of product need in a location with Internet sales there. We were fortunate that Marc and Vinnie from Diapers.com were willing to let us examine all their US sales data.

Our thesis was pretty simple. In locations where people with young kids requiring diapers and formula and so on are relatively few in number, *percentagewise*, their offline options won't be that great.

Why?

Well, if retailers want to make money (most do) then they aren't going to pay much attention to product categories and brands that relatively few people in their trading area are after.

Now back to that field trip.

Before spending literally months writing programs and running computer models on a lot of data, we wanted to get an advance check on whether our basic idea had any merit. It felt intuitive, but we couldn't be sure before we did at least a bit of investigating.

So, we went online (where else!) in order to identify retailers in the Philadelphia area who (a) had stores in more than one location, and (b) sold baby-related products like diapers and formula and so on. Our search identified two major chains, Fresh Grocer and Walmart, who had three and two stores respectively within an easy drive of the Penn campus.

In addition to considering stores in more than one zip code, we also needed to make sure that the percentage of households with children

---

14 For details, see http://www.esri.com/data/find-data.

varied across the zip codes in our field study. That is, we needed some variation in the "preference isolation" status of families in Philadelphia who had children and lived in different locations.

So, back to the US Census.

We noted that in the zip codes in which the Fresh Grocer stores were located the fractions of households with children aged six and under varied from about 10.6 percent to 16.3 percent.[15] One of the Walmart stores was located in a zip with 13.9 percent young kids, whereas the other had 19.9 percent.

Our plan of attack was simple.

We would drive over to those stores, go to the baby aisle, and count the number of diaper packs they were selling, both in total and individually for each of the three leading brands: Pampers, Huggies, and Luvs.

Our theory was very simple as well.

If the "preference isolation" concept actually works in real markets, we expected to find that the stores in neighborhoods in which around 10 percent of the population had children would have fewer packs of diapers and less variety than stores in neighborhoods in which 15 to 20 percent of the households had children. That is, we expected to see that real-world retailers have some understanding of who is in their trading areas and adjust their assortments accordingly. This is actually a pretty reasonable assumption and there is good academic research to support it.[16]

I rarely do data collection "in the field," so to speak, and perhaps I should do more of it. This particular effort was somewhere between mildly embarrassing, as we were armed with pink measuring tape, and somewhat exhilarating, as we skillfully dodged store managers. (Phila-

---

15 In an ideal world, we'd know the exact percentages of children still in diapers, but for our purposes knowing the percentage under six is a good proxy. This is because it captures relative differences *across* zip codes. If one zip code has 15 percent of the population under six and another has 10 percent, then the first zip code will almost surely have more children under two as well. Also, the nice thing about our idea is that it can be implemented with "decent" data—it certainly does not require exactitude. Or if you prefer, it does not require "certitude" (a favored word of one-time New York City mayoral candidate Anthony Weiner).

16 See, for example, Yuxin Chen, James Hess, Ronald Wilcox, and Z. John Zhang, "Accounting Profits Versus Marketing Profits: A Relevant Metric for Category Management," *Marketing Science* 18, no. 3 (August 1999), 208–29.

delphia is, after all, the town that booed Santa Claus,[17] so it was hard to know how area managers would react to foreigners with a pink measuring tape checking out the size of the diaper assortments in their stores.)

Our little exercise confirmed our hunch.

In the stores for which the census told us that there were more babies nearby than in other zip codes, retailers had allocated more space to the diaper category. One nice thing about our small experiment was that the stores in the same chain all had the same approximate "footprint" in terms of square footage, so the *total* amount of space to be allocated to all product categories was the same across all markets.

PRACTICALITIES OF PREFERENCE ISOLATION—NO VEGEMITE FOR YOU

Before I share the results from our statistical analysis, let's again build up the preference isolation concept by example.

Imagine, for the moment, that you and I both have young children, but that we live in different neighborhoods. Also, and very important, imagine that there is *exactly the same* number of kids in my neighborhood and in yours. To keep things simple, let's say that there are one hundred households with babies in both locations.

There is, however, a key difference—there are two hundred households in total in your location while there are one thousand in mine. In your location, people with young babies are everywhere—they are literally 50 percent (100/200) of the neighborhood. In my location, people with babies are somewhat of a rarity, accounting for only 10 percent (100/1,000) of the population overall.

Now, since we both have one hundred kids in our locations, there will be the same *total* need for diapers in both locations. What will differ, however, by the theory of preference isolation, is the amount of diaper demand that is fulfilled in the real world versus the virtual world.

Central place theory tells us that there will be more stores in my

17 Lest you find this completely unbelievable, here is the documented proof: E. J. Dickson, "The *New York Times* Can't Stop Trolling Philadelphia," *Salon*, June 13, 2013, www.salon.com/2013/06/13/the_new_york_times_cant_stop_trolling_philadelphia/.

neighborhood because my neighborhood has more people. To keep things simple, let's imagine that the number of stores is proportional to the population—a pretty robust and not unreasonable assumption. Specifically, that there is a single store in your location and five stores in mine, since my location has five times the total population.

One thing that's true in the real world is that store sizes for a particular chain don't change that much according to location (the size of a Target, Fresh Grocer, and so on is pretty much constant regardless of where it is located).

Again, to keep the math simple and to illuminate the idea, let's see what the manager of that single store in your neighborhood does with his shelf space. Let's imagine that he has a store of two hundred square feet (this is of course a bit small, but it's only an example, and we want to keep the math easy). Since he notices that half of the people in his trading area have children, he might reasonably allocate half of his store to diapers and baby-related products.[18]

So, in your neighborhood there is a single store with one hundred of out of two hundred total square feet allocated to diapers and baby-related products. That means that the assortment should be pretty decent, the prices quite reasonable, and so on.

Over in my neighborhood, things are not quite so rosy. There are five stores, but the managers are willing to allocate only twenty square feet in each store (or 10 percent of the store) to baby-related products. Again, managers are doing something quite reasonable—allocating scarce shelf space to products according to the proportion of target customers that want them. As a result, each store in my neighborhood has a pretty basic selection—they all carry Pampers in a few different sizes and varieties and perhaps a few other things, but the selection is nowhere near as good as it is for you.

This idea is kind of cool in that (1) the total number of potential customers in each market is *the same*, (2) the total demand for the product

---

18 Whether or not he *actually* sets aside half of his store for baby products isn't important. All that matters is that the amount of space allocated for them should: (1) be proportional to the size of the target population, and (2) be greater in your neighborhood than in mine. Jeonghye and I found that both of these things were true after visiting real stores in Philadelphia.

in each market is therefore *the same*, (3) the managers allocate the same *total* amount of space to the product category, and yet, as we will see (and as might already be clear), the amount of demand being served by the virtual world in the two markets will be very different.

Specifically, sellers in the virtual world of the Internet have a lot of pull over me, because those in the real world are not giving me what I need. In short, I am a *preference minority* because I want things (baby-related items in this case) that most of my neighbors simply don't want, and this leads to my poor treatment in the real world.

I've included a picture of elements (1)–(3) as figure 5.1 just to help you keep track, and to help you think about how to apply the concept to other product categories and contexts! For example, the most extreme form of preference isolation is one in which the desired product or service is not offered at all in the real world, rather than just in limited variety. In all the years I've lived in Philadelphia, I've yet to find Vegemite on the shelf of my local Fresh Grocer store.

HOW SELLERS BENEFIT FROM ISOLATED CUSTOMERS

We gathered together all the sales data from Diapers.com and tested our theory that demand would be higher in locations in which the target customers—households with young children—were relatively rare and therefore probably "isolated" in their preferences. We were curious to see if our ideas about how real-world isolation affected virtual-world buying behavior actually held water.

The statistical results were striking. If we took two different locations—one where the percentage of households with babies was 10 percent (like mine in the example), and one where the percentage of babies was 20 percent (closer to yours in the example), demand for Diapers.com was 50 percent higher in my location! (In the real world, the variation is not quite the 10 to 50 percent in the example summarized in figure 5.1, but more like 10 to 20 percent.)

As always, these analyses involve everything else being held equal. That's the beauty of statistical analysis. We can control for other things that differ across locations, such as the population age, size, income,

Figure 5.1

Preference Isolation and Geographic Differences in Shelf Space Allocation

Target Population	Total Population	Target Population as Proportion of Total[1]	Stores (200 sq ft each) and Category Shelf Space per Store[2]	Total Shelf Space per Market[3]
Market A				
100	200	100 / 200 = 50%	 100	100 sq ft
Market B				
100	1,000	100 / 1,000 = 10%	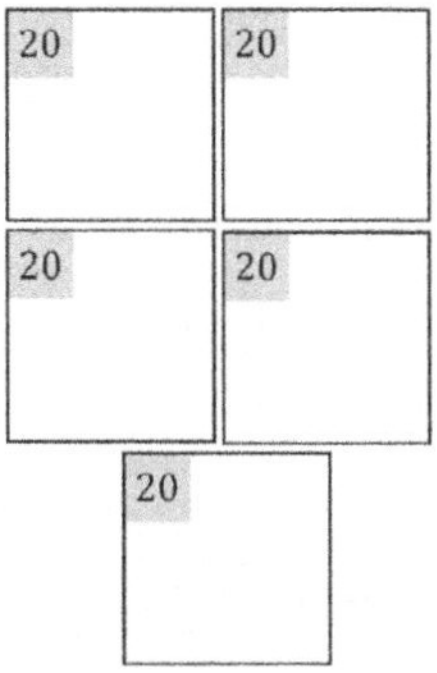 20 20 / 20 20 / 20	100 sq ft

Notes

[1] Markets A and B both have 100 residents in the target population, e.g., households with babies. Since Market B has a larger population, the target customers in Market B are, relatively speaking, preference minorities.

[2] Stores are the same size (200 square feet) in both markets, however market B has five times as many stores because it has a larger total population (in the text we use US market data to show that while the number of stores increases with the population size, the size of the stores from a given chain does not). Stores allocate shelf space to categories in proportion to the size of the target market for that category, i.e., the store in Market A allocates 50% while each store in Market B allocates 10%.

[3] The *aggregate* shelf space allocated to the category is the same in the two markets; however, the *assortment per store* will be much greater in Market A.

number of stores, and so on, and just focus on the one key effect that we are interested in.

It wasn't simply the case that there were more people or households with babies *in total* in my location. Just as in the motivating example, our locations were identical in all practical regards save one: the percentage of households with babies. And in the ways that they didn't quite match, we accounted for this with a statistical model.[19]

In addition to finding that virtual-world demand at Diapers.com was much greater in markets with isolated customers, we also found that customers suffering from preference isolation were relatively price-insensitive.[20] Because their offline shopping costs are already pretty high (it's difficult to downright impossible for them to get what they want locally), they are willing to pay a bit more when they shop online. This price sensitivity finding is of course very good news for sellers.

Our study also found important differences between sales of popular products (such as Pampers, the market leader) and niche products (like Seventh Generation, an environmentally-friendly brand). Your intuition probably helps here. If, due to my preference isolation for baby-related products, I am having a hard time getting access to a good variety of Pampers products at decent prices, then finding Seventh Generation products will probably be tougher still!

And that is exactly what we found.

So, in summary, the overall effect of preference isolation is very large. In markets whose customers are really suffering, relatively speaking, from preference isolation (those at the ninetieth percentile on the isolation scale) online sales are about 50 percent higher compared with locations that have an identical number of customers but where preference isolation is not prevalent.

In a further twist, we found that this overall category effect is amplified for individual niche brands. While the leading brand (Pampers) gets a virtual-world sales boost of about 40 percent in preference mi-

---

19 For those of you who care about the details, markets where 20 percent of the households had babies were located at the very low end, at about the tenth percentile, on the "isolation scale." Households with children were quite common in those markets and therefore not very isolated at all. Conversely, markets where only 10 percent of the households had babies were up at the ninetieth percentile on the "isolation scale." In other words, people with babies were, relatively speaking, quite rare in these markets.

20 We were able to test this by using the fact that the discrepancy between online tax rates (typically zero) and offline tax rates varied across different zip codes. The bigger the discrepancy, the more favorable the *effective online price* is. We found that customers who were suffering from preference isolation were less responsive to more favorable effective online prices (i.e., they would buy online anyway), and were therefore less price sensitive.

nority locations, a niche brand like Seventh Generation can see a sales lift of up to 140 percent.

So, the Long Tail comes into play here as well.

In chapter 4, VICINITY, I introduced the Spatial Long Tail to illustrate the collective importance of locations with relatively low individual demand, but didn't relate this concept to sales of particular brands. I'll do that now.

We found that niche brands (in the "tail") get a very high proportion of their online sales from preference minority locations, whereas leading brands draw sales more evenly from across the country. So that means that a virtual-world seller can *really* capitalize by selling niche brands to customers who reside in preference minority *locations*.

So, there's a subtle point here when we connect the preference isolation effect to virtual-world demand for specific types of brands, i.e., popular brands and niche brands.

Customers who are preference minorities are, by definition, starved of variety in their real-world options. In their locations even relatively "popular" items (think Pampers again) may only be offered in limited sizes or variants, or may run out of stock. So if securing a popular item is tough, it's doubly (or more so) for niche items.

What we have is a bit of a marriage made in heaven. If you're a seller and you can find customers who are isolated *and* who want niche or long tail products as well, demand from them will be very high. Customers will be happy, and also relatively price-insensitive—which is a winning combination for sellers. In chapter 2, RESISTANCE, we saw that the benefit of buying online depends a lot on where a person lives. In this chapter we added another very important condition: It's not only where we live but *who* we live next to as well that matters for our choices. If the majority of those who live next to you are too different in characteristics or stage of life or preferences, then you'll be a preference minority and turn to the virtual world for liberation.

Summary

On average, we share characteristics with others in our locations, but that doesn't mean that our preferences will always coincide with those of our neighbors. Perhaps we have children, yet all our neighbors are elderly. Perhaps we go on a health kick and turn vegan, but there are no suitable restaurants or stores in our neighborhood. So, our neighbors are either helping us to get what we want, or preventing that from happening! In the real world, isolation deflates and dictates that you're not going to get what you want.

Furthermore, in the real world, product variety is targeted. There have to be sufficient numbers of people needing a certain good or service, or it just doesn't get offered locally at all. Being in a "bigger" location doesn't necessarily help either, if your tastes are too uncommon. At times it can be advantageous to shield your identity and blend in with the majority, and if your choices are publicly visible, then you might just acquiesce and go with what others are doing.

So, for virtual-world sellers our status with respect to *local others* is of critical importance. Virtual-world sellers have a more difficult time competing with real-world sellers offering mainstream products. Instead, they should focus on target locations in which potential customers form a preference minority. These customers have high offline searching and shopping costs, and are therefore not price sensitive.

As a result, a disproportionate amount of demand for a virtual-world seller comes from "preference minority" locations—as the Diapers.com example showed. Two locations could have an identical amount of *total* demand for a product category, but if in one market the customer group was a relatively small fraction of the total population, online demand in that location could be up to 50 percent higher. For niche brands, this effect gets amplified and can exceed 100 percent.

Isolation offline becomes liberation online. You'll succeed by identifying, serving, and investing in the isolated.

Six

TOPOGRAPHY

The Evolving Landscape of the Real and Virtual Worlds: People, Information, and Goods in Play and on the Move

TO·POG·RA·PHY *n.*
The arrangement of the natural and artificial physical features of an area.

I began this book by explaining some fundamentals about geography and about how the real world evolved as it did, from the perspective of individual location choices and the products and services that spring up in different markets. In chapter 1 (GEOGRAPHY), I also spent a bit of time on some surprising facts about how location choice not only constrains our product choices and our needs for information, but also starts to actually shape them as well. Remember: You prefer Budweiser in Missouri and Coors in Colorado. And Folgers bests Maxwell House in San Francisco, but not in Boston! New Yorkers spend more time scouring for local information that Iowans do.

In chapter 2 (RESISTANCE), I took us on a tour through the two main frictions that the real world puts in our way — search friction and geographic friction — and looked at how the virtual world helps us overcome them. Next, in chapters 3 (ADJACENCY), 4 (VICINITY), and 5 (ISOLATION), we studied the effects of real-world location on virtual-world demand in a systematic and progressively nuanced and focused way.

In this last chapter I bring things full circle.

Many of us are now enjoying a seamless TOPOGRAPHY in which real-world/virtual-world interaction is the norm.

We consult Yelp for crowd-sourced reviews before eating, check Google Maps or Waze to find the best route home, and order a shaving kit from Harrys.com while waiting in line at Dunkin' Donuts (before paying for our coffee with their app!). Of particular note are all of the *location-based* activities we engage in with our virtual-world devices (smartphones, tablets, and so on). According to Pew Research, the vast majority of US consumers with smartphones use them to obtain location-based information.[1]

In this chapter I present new ideas and findings about these overlapping landscapes, or topographies, of our two worlds, and how they're merging ever closer, providing one integrated experience for searchers, shoppers, and sellers worldwide.

People Populating the Real-World/ Virtual-World Landscapes

It's quite astounding to watch the clock at the US Census's website as it indicates a birth every 8 seconds and a death every 12 seconds![2] The real-world population keeps expanding, and the virtual-world one does too.[3] Internet penetration is about 35 percent on average, with the most-penetrated countries (these include Germany, Japan, Korea, the United Kingdom, and the United States) at around 80 percent or above.[4]

So even though the virtual world is ubiquitous, not everyone in the

---

1 For more details, see the data available at the Pew Research Center's website: http://pewinternet .org/Commentary/2012/February/Pew-Internet-Mobile.aspx.

2 The clock may be seen at www.census.gov/popclock.

3 This number comes from http://internetworldstats.com/. For those who enjoy facts and figures, there is a wealth of information at this site as well as at http://www.census.gov/pop clock/. From what I can tell, Australia and New Zealand actually have the highest rates of Internet penetration in the world, at about 88 percent, while obviously contributing a miniscule proportion of the total worldwide membership of the virtual world (less than 0.5 percent).

4 Internet World Stats, Usage and Population Stats, Miniwatts Marketing Group, 2012, http:// internetworldstats.com/top20.htm.

real world, or within a country, has equal access to it. As a result, government agencies, nonprofits, and large firms are among those doing what they can to bring the virtual world to everyone. Google, for example, launched Project Loon under the umbrella Google X in the South Island of New Zealand, with the goal of bringing Internet everywhere in the world, via radio-carrying balloons.[5]

On a global scale, Internet penetration (and virtual-world membership) is positively correlated with economic factors, such as gross national product. It is also interesting to note that Internet penetration *contributes* to GDP, in the sense that countries with more connection to the virtual world enjoy all kinds of efficiencies, cutting-edge business models, and so on.[6] That's of course another reason why it's so important for everyone to have access to the virtual world.

As I mentioned in chapter 1 (GEOGRAPHY), the inhabitants of the real and virtual worlds are also still quite distinct *within* a country as well as among countries. In the United States, for example, the digital divide means that minorities and those with lower incomes and education levels have less access to the virtual world than others do, although the gap is shrinking. Recent research does show, however, that upon access to the virtual world, (some) minorities spend more time there (more statistics in a moment).

The Digital Divide Revisited

Early in the book, I shared some ideas about the topography of the real world. For example, the principle of Tiebout sorting explains how neighborhoods form and who lives in them, and central place theory helps us understand what goods and services spring up to serve these locations.

The virtual world, just like the real one, is a large collection of many

---

5 http://www.popsci.com/technology/article/2013-06/google-wants-carry-connectivity-around-world-balloons.

6 A recent report by the consulting firm McKinsey & Company illuminates many of the details on this interesting issue. See Matthieu Pélissié du Rausas, James Manyika, Eric Hazan, Jacques Bughin, Michael Chui, and Rémi Said, "Internet Matters: The Net's Sweeping Impact on Growth, Jobs, and Prosperity," McKinsey Global Institute, May 2011.

smaller neighborhoods. In most countries, the profile of the average person who is active in the virtual world is a bit different than that of the average person in real-world neighborhoods.

In fact, US data (for example) show just that.

According to researchers at the University of Chicago, ethnicity impacts the likelihood that you're online, or in the virtual world, to begin with.[7] If you're black, then you are about 4 percent *less* likely to be online than if you are white; if you're Asian then you are 3 percent *more* likely to be online.

Not only that, but if you're black, then you're about 10 percent less likely than a member of another group to *buy* something online. This leads to a kind of double jeopardy. African Americans are less likely to participate in the virtual world to begin with and less likely to transact business there when they do participate.

As you might expect, older citizens are present in fewer numbers in the virtual world than younger people are. There's no noticeable trend for gender, with men and women equally active online, on average, although this does of course vary by site and product category.

Shopper Frictions on Fixed Versus Mobile Devices

One of the most important things shaping the topography of commerce in both worlds is the steady move by shoppers and sellers from fixed Internet-connected devices (desktops and laptops) to mobile ones (smartphones, feature phones, tablets, and so on). I'm using "fixed" to mean desktops and laptops because while laptops are of course movable, consumers typically don't use them (literally) while moving about, and, more important, a mobile device is more likely to be connected to just *one* single user.

Effects of this shift in device usage on the two critical frictions — search and geographic — that we discussed in chapter 2 (RESISTANCE) are especially strong. Researchers from New York, Toronto, and Hong Kong (a nice international team) demonstrated this using Korean

---

7 Ethan Lieber and Chad Syverson, "Online Versus Offline Competition" in *The Oxford Handbook of the Digital Economy*, ed. Martin Peitz and Joel Waldfogel (New York: Oxford University Press, 2011), 189–223.

"Twitter-like" data from a large sample of users.[8] They wanted to know whether browsing behavior and the effect of frictions differ when we use fixed versus mobile devices.

Before giving you the key findings, I want to share a little bit of background research on what is known about browsing behavior in general.

Imagine that you're searching via Google for things to do during an upcoming vacation in Los Angeles. (Lucky you—who among us could object to a weekend in the City of Angels?)

You need somewhere to stay, so you search the term "Hotels in LA." Google returns a list of results. The first three at the top of the page and those down the right hand side of the page are labeled as ads (you're into fine print, so you mouse over the information icon above the ads and see "these ads are based on your current search terms").

Below the ads are the top "organic links," that is, the links to the sites that Google thinks will be the most helpful to you. In contrast, for sponsored links, the basic idea is that the link that shows up first is the link that Google thinks is the best fit for you, *after* taking into account what a seller has bid for the terms so that its link gets shown to you.[9]

So how do you (and I) respond to these sponsored ad links?

Well, the first link is typically the one most likely to be clicked on, the second the second most likely, and so on. So the seller with the highest rank in the paid search process gets the best response or, in industry language for the most common metric for measuring response, the best click-through rate (CTR).

So, for the *same* search, "Hotels in LA," is there a difference between links being clicked on from fixed devices versus links getting clicked on from mobile phones?

Well, on a fixed device like a laptop, one move up in the ranking delivers a 25 percent lift in the CTR. Let's do some simple math to see this. If the chance that you click on the link ranked second is 10 percent then the chance that you click on the top link is 12.5 percent, or 25 percent

---

8 Anindya Ghose, Avi Goldfarb, and Sang Pil Han, "How Is the Mobile Internet Different? Search Costs and Local Activities," *Information Systems Research* 24, no. 3 (September 2013), 613–31.

9 I won't go into all the details here, but if you want to watch a cute video by Google chief economist Hal Varian in which he explains how the ad auction works for sponsored or paid search, and what ends up in what position, visit www.youtube.com/watch?v=a8qQXLby4PY.

more. (Of course, real-life CTRs are way lower than this, but you get the point.)

So in search, as in life, it is generally better to be ranked first than second, second than third, and so on. Bear in mind of course that the *cost* to the seller goes up as well—you have to bid more on the search terms if you want to come out on top.[10]

So we know there's a "rank premium" of 25 percent on fixed devices. What about on mobile devices? Is it the same, more, or less?

If you said "more," you've got good instincts.

The researchers found that moving up one position in the ranking *increased* the click-through rate by 37 percent, a lift of about 50 percent over what happens on the fixed devices, for exactly the *same* kinds of ads. Going back to our earlier example, we find that if the CTR for the second position is 10 percent, then for the top position it's 13.7 percent.

This is a really whopping effect! Going mobile *increases* your virtual-world search friction, because you're *less* likely to click on the lower-ranked links and there's a higher lift for the higher-ranked links.

Now what about geographic friction?

Well, when you're searching for local stores and brands on your fixed Internet device, a one-mile decrease between where you are and where the store is *increases* the CTR by about 12 percent. Let's go back to my beer example in the introduction to see how this works. If while sitting at home I type "buy beer in Philadelphia," I observe the following.

The first two listings are hawthornecafe.com, or Hawthornes (which turns out to be a "Beer Boutique and Gourmet Eatery" and looks outstanding by the way), and stonesofphilly.com, or Stone's Beverage Center. Hawthornes is about 2.7 miles from my apartment, whereas Stone's Beverage Center is about 1.6 miles away. So let's say that Stone's is about one mile closer.

If I were searching on my MacBook, everything else being equal

---

10 For some really fascinating insights on how to bid for keywords in Google auctions, I encourage you to take a look at Bernd Skiera and Nadia Abou Nabout, "PROSAD: A Bidding Decision Support System for Profit Optimizing Search Engine Advertising," *Marketing Science* 32, no. 2 (March–April 2013), 213–20. You can also watch the authors present their ideas in a video at the MIT site: http://techtv.mit.edu/videos/18315-prosad. They make a rather compelling case that most advertisers bid too much (and place too much emphasis on getting a "high position") and would run more profitable campaigns by bidding *less* and ending up in lower positions.

(there's that phrase again), I'd be about 12 percent more likely to click on the closer store—i.e., Stone's instead of Hawthornes—simply because it's a mile closer to me. And as we all know by now, things that are closer are more attractive, or exert more pull over us, thanks to gravity.

The researchers found that searching on a mobile device *doubles* the "one mile premium." Using my iPhone, I'd be about 23 percent more likely to click on the Hawthornes link. So, using a mobile device *increases* geographic friction, because it makes closer things even more attractive to us.

Let's think about this for a moment.

The two findings, taken together, yield an intriguing implication, especially when we connect them back to our discussion in chapter 2 (RESISTANCE).There we noted that one of the great things about the Internet, in general, is that it *reduces* search friction. Instead of visiting all those hotels in LA, or calling them to find out about rates and amenities, you can just get the price and other information you need online. Similarly, it *reduces* geographic friction because you can access goods and information beyond what's simply offered locally.

And yet, mobile devices *increase* search and geographic frictions, relative to those experienced when using fixed Internet devices.

So what's the explanation? The increased rank premium or increase in search friction is due to the size of the device. The screen is smaller, so lower-ranked results are more difficult to access. The increased distance premium or increase in geographic friction is due to the shopper or searcher's "state" or mind-set that's most likely when a mobile Internet-connected device is in use. If I'm searching for beer at home, I could be in the mood to buy it or simply just checking around. If I'm searching for beer on my iPhone, I am more likely to be either out and about or in the mood to buy it right then and there. As such, I pay more attention to which stores are closest to me.

Five "Rules" of Mobile

While the friction results are very interesting, there are other key differences to keep in mind when considering the effects of fixed versus Internet devices as well. My friend Rob Coneybeer is a specialist investor in Internet startups, and he has some great insights into how the use of mobile devices changes real-world/virtual-world connections.[11]

According to Rob, the mobile Internet, relative to fixed Internet, has five critical features that are going to dramatically alter searching, shopping, and selling. In order to make this point to my class, Rob started by taking out his iPhone and adjusting the temperature in his apartment. He has a Nest thermostat (http://nest.com) in his house that is controlled with his phone. He quipped that he wondered how long his family members would take before they realized it was getting a bit hotter at home.

So, what are the five rules?

First, mobile has what Rob calls "instant-on." There is no delay to getting into a searching or shopping context, as consumers can "snack" all the time. Wherever we are in the real world, we can be using our "dead time" to participate in the virtual one: On the subway, on the walk to the office, and of course in class (although I hope not too much in mine!). The mobile device also plays into (and furthers) our increasingly shorter attention spans. According to the Pew Research Center, almost nine out of ten teachers thought that connected devices were leading students to be more distracted and display shorter attention spans.[12]

Second, sensors on the device allow us to take photos, share videos, and of course communicate location information. Some of the most interesting recent innovations, like the Waze app for "Outsmarting traffic, together" (www.waze.com), rely on this functionality. Third—and perhaps more controversially—the mobile device is the domain of apps. There's evidence that we are all starting to prefer native apps to mobile sites (by that I mean versions of websites configured for mobile devices). For example, my preferred way to book a flight on United Airlines is through their great iPhone app. Real-world symbols are still important here, so for sellers it's key to create exactly the right "Chiclet icon" to sit on our phones and yell out to be used!

11 To learn more about what Rob does, check out www.shastaventures.com/team/rob_coney beer or follow him on @robconeybeer. The observations that follow are based on Rob's seminar, titled "Mobile Marketing," which was given at the Wharton School in my Digital Marketing and E-commerce course.

12 For more information, see this excellent article in the *Guardian*: Duncan Jefferies, "Is Technology and the Internet Reducing Pupils' Attention Spans?," March 11, 2013, www.theguardian .com/teacher-network/teacher-blog/2013/mar/11/technology-internet-pupil-attention- teaching.

Fourth, at no time in human history, have more people been con-nected to a device that is essentially a distribution channel (for product and content) connected to a payment system. And the number is only going to increase. No wonder we're all getting pretty impulsive when it comes to searching and shopping!

Back in chapter 3 (ADJACENCY), I demonstrated the power of word of mouth among adjacent individuals and locations. Well, mobile de-vices greatly amplify the power of word of mouth. Instead of just telling you about the Hotel Tonight app, I can take out my iPhone and *show* you how it works. That's Rob's fifth and final point — show and tell, as he did by turning up the heat on his family via iPhone and Nest, is a com-pelling way to spread the word.

WHO IS KNOWN AND WHO WANTS TO BE KNOWN

Popularity on the Rise and Organic Celebrity

Another fascinating thing that's happening as the real and virtual worlds merge, and the new topography unfolds, is the blurring of lines between traditional and new forms of celebrity. Increasingly, many of us are building our own personal brands and being ever more public in various social forums. So who are the real-world individuals most popular in the virtual one?

A tantalizingly titled article gets right to the point. Researchers in Germany, the United Kingdom, and Brazil (there's that international collaborative effort again) published "Measuring User Influence in Twitter: The Million Follower Fallacy," which presented an "in-depth comparison of three measures of influence."[13]

First up, here are the three measures: (1) the number of followers, (2) the number of mentions, and (3) the number of retweets. The au-thors were not deterred by the colossal amount of data available on

---

13 Meeyoung Cha, Hamed, Haddadi, Fabrício Benevenuto, and Krishna Gummadi, "Meas-uring User Influence in Twitter: The Million Follower Fallacy," Proceedings of the Fourth International AAAI Conference on Weblogs and Social Media (Association for the Ad-vancement of Artificial Intelligence, 2010), www.aaai.org/ocs/index.php/ICWSM/ICWSM 10/paper/view/1538.

Twitter, as they looked at over 2 billion "follow" links, i.e., instances of one person following another on Twitter, among about 54 million users.

Here's what they found.

The number of followers one has is a broad measure of high-level fame. People who are famous (Shaquille O'Neal, Barack Obama) tend to have what is known more technically as "high Indegree" (just a fancy term for a concentration of followers), or, in other words, a large audience for whatever it is that they happen to say.

Retweets measure how good the stuff you say or put out there actually is. If you have good content, then you get retweeted. The top retweeted "users" tend to be news aggregators rather than individuals per se and include Mashable and the *New York Times*.

The third measure is "mentions," which are indicative of popularity related to liking or positive affect. That is, if people feel good about you or just otherwise like you, you might nab a few mentions. The most mentioned individuals on Twitter tend to be celebrities of some stripe or another (musicians, actors, models, and so on).

All three virtual-world measures are quite distinct and reflect different kinds of real-world status. Only two people were in the top twenty of all three metrics at the time of the study—Ashton Kutcher and Sean "Puff Daddy" Combs. These gentlemen have fame, interesting content, and appear to be well liked.

A winning combination indeed!

When the researchers looked at patterns in the data they found that the correlation between the retweets and mentions was much stronger than the correlation between either of these measures and the measure of "general fame," the number of followers.[14]

What does this mean?

---

14 The correlation between retweets and mentions is over .60 among the top 1 percent and top 10 percent of users on Twitter. So for these subpopulations there is a strong positive association. Conversely, the correlation between either of these measures and Indegree is roughly between .10 and .30, which means that the positive association is much lower, barely even there. There's also a technical reason for focusing on the top 10 percent of users and above. When the researchers look at *all* users on Twitter, many of us have very low numbers of retweets, followers, and mentions. If all our data were included, this would artificially inflate the correlations. That's because the correlation between a long list of zeros (mentions for most regular account holders on Twitter) and another long list of zeros (retweets for most regular account holders on Twitter) would, after all, be equal to one.

It means that general fame *per se* as measured by number of followers might not be that helpful in generating engagement in the virtual world. So if you're an Internet seller and you want to enlist a celebrity to promote your brand or business, it's best to find someone with a highly engaged fan base. Such fans have a strong affinity with the celebrity and are highly connected to him or her.

Individuals who fit this characterization now abound in all kinds of product categories and interest groups. Two good people to illustrate this new kind of organic celebrity are Michelle Phan, who rose to fame and her own brand through authentic engagement with cosmetics, and Ree Drummond, who describes herself in the following delightful way: "I'm a desperate housewife. I live in the country. I channel Lucille Ball, Vivien Leigh, and Ethel Merman. Welcome to my frontier!"

Here's a cute insight from a separate piece of research conducted at Columbia University. For this particular study, the authors recruited enterprising undergraduate students and instructed them to generate fake followers for real users on Twitter.[15] The goal was to examine how real users react when they notice increases in their number of followers. Specifically, the goal was to understand exactly what motivates users on Twitter—people like you and me—to get involved with this medium at all. Just what does it mean to us to have people follow us, mention us, or retweet our 140 (or less) characters of insight?

The researchers used some clever mathematics to tease out two different types of motivation and to measure them from the data. The first kind of motivation is *extrinsic*. Extrinsic motivations are related to ego. We just like the idea of more fans (followers) and get what academics call "image-related utility" from building up a fan base. We feel good about ourselves because people want to follow us!

The second kind of motivation is *intrinsic*. This kind of motivation is far more altruistic—our goal is primarily to help others through the sharing of our insights and information.

In turns out that there's strong evidence for both types of motivation among typical Twitter users. However, ego and image-related mo-

---

15 For more details on the study, and the procedure as well, see Oliver Toubia and Andrew Stephen, "Intrinsic vs. Image-Related Utility in Social Media: Why Do People Contribute Content to Twitter?," *Marketing Science* 32, no. 3 (May–June 2013), 368–92. If you want to try this out, then go to http://www.fakenamegenerator.com/.

tivations tend to be more common than altruistic ones. For most of us, about 75 percent of the weight is on extrinsic motivation and only 25 percent is on sharing helpful insights with others.

Knowing Me, Knowing You (Is There Nothing We Can Do)?

While most of us are engaged in the virtual world sharing all kinds of real-world happenings, privacy concerns are an important part of this new topography. We all have a different level of tolerance with respect to how much of ourselves we want "out there" in both worlds, and how much we want others—sellers in particular—to know about us.

Some fascinating research by scholars at MIT and the University of Toronto shows where society seems to be heading on privacy. They set out to understand how consumers felt about different sellers' tactics for advertising in the virtual world.[16]

We've all seen a lot of display advertising. It all started, so the story goes, in 1994, when HotWired.com sold so-called banner advertising to AT&T.[17]

As of 2013, about $12 billion per year goes into banner advertising, but there's a lot of disagreement about how effective it is. That's because the associated CTRs are just so low. Of the many skeptical assessments, one of my favorites is the "10 Horrifying Stats About Display Advertising," compiled by HubSpot in 2013. Number one is especially good—apparently you and I are more likely to complete a Navy Seal training program than we are to click on a banner ad.[18]

Nevertheless, sellers pour more than $12 billion into this marketing tool every year in the United States alone, so it has to be doing *something*.

After analyzing the results of over three thousand campaigns and

---

16 Avi Goldfarb and Catherine Tucker, "Online Display Advertising: Targeting and Obtrusiveness," *Marketing Science* 30, no. 3 (May–June 2011), 389–404.

17 For a helpful history see http://en.wikipedia.org/wiki/HotWired.

18 Mike Volpe, "10 Horrifying Stats About Display Advertising," HubSpot, April 29, 2013, http://blog.hubspot.com/marketing/horrifying-display-advertising-stats. On the other hand, some of these ads are really cool and would seem to justify some attention. Check out Todd Wasserman, "10 Insanely Clickable Banner Ads," Mashable, May 28, 2012, http://mashable .com/2012/05/28/10-insanely-clickable-banner-ads/.

surveying random samples of people exposed to those campaigns, the researchers discovered two very interesting things. First, certain kinds of execution improved the CTRs. Specifically, ads that were more "obtrusive" got more clicks. That is, ads that moved, popped up, popped down, utilized video, and so on just got more attention.

Next the researchers looked at ads that were "contextually targeted" and found that they got more CTRs too. Contextually targeted means that the content of the ad matched the content of the site. To borrow an example from the authors: "A banner ad for a cruise would be a *contextually targeted ad* if it was displayed on a site devoted to travel and leisure."[19]

So, obtrusiveness works (more CTRs).

Contextual targeting does too (more CTRs as well).

That's the first finding.

The second finding tweaks this first one in a somewhat disturbing way (if you're a seller, anyway). While obtrusiveness and contextual targeting work individually, doing them *at the same time* is not a good idea. In technical or statistical terms, the *interaction effect* of doing both at once is negative and therefore *reduces* click-through rates and effectiveness.

Why?

This is because consumers feel that they are being manipulated when relevant ads (contextually targeted) are now more "in your face" (obtrusive) as well. Some alarm bells go off that the seller knows too much and that consumers' privacy could be in jeopardy. Consumer aversion to these virtual-world advertising messages was also connected to their real-world characteristics as well.

After surmising that privacy concerns were the root cause of the negative interaction effect between obtrusiveness and contextual targeting, the researchers started looking more deeply at *who* the ad recipients were and *what* they were looking for online. Among all consumers who filled in surveys that measured how they responded to the ads, those who refused to answer an income-related question showed the largest negative interaction effect. That is, when they saw ads that were contextually targeted and obtrusive, their response went way down.

---

19 Goldfarb and Tucker, "Online Display Advertising."

Real world characteristics matter a lot—if you don't like giving your income category in an anonymous survey then you're probably among the more paranoid of ad recipients! So, that's the *who*. The *what* was important too. Shoppers who were looking for information about health and financial services products also showed big negative reactions to advertising that was obtrusive and targeted.

Information in the Real-World/ Virtual-World Landscape

Throughout the book I've treated information and goods separately, and I will keep that distinction going. In the new topography, information formats and flows are critical to the way the real and virtual worlds will evolve together to facilitate and serve shopping, searching, and selling.

WHAT INFORMATION, WHICH SOURCE, AND FROM WHOM TO WHOM

In chapter 1 (GEOGRAPHY) I introduced the concept of social capital — the extent to which people trust and interact with each other in real-world communities. I'm going back to that in more depth now, because it has a lot to say about how frequently people converse and whether they believe what is said. I'll walk through two examples that have important implications for sellers.

Hey, I Like Your Peacock Pants!

My coauthor Jae Young Lee and I were curious to see how real-world social capital would influence the sales of a virtual-world company. Specifically, we were interested in the effect on a company selling products with "experience attributes," or "touch and feel" components—things like fashion apparel and so on. You don't really know what a shirt or skirt or pair of pants will look and feel like until you try them on. This uncertainty can prevent consumers from taking the plunge and actually buying these things online.

This uncertainty is a well-known obstacle to buying in the virtual world, so sellers do creative things to help consumers feel better. Zappos.com, the famous shoe seller, pioneered "two-way free shipping," and this is now de rigueur in e-commerce. The fashion eyewear seller WarbyParker.com offers a "home try-on" program in which customers get five frames for five days to try at home for free.

Now, since the social capital landscape varies a lot from one location to the next, we wanted to see if this variation would affect virtual-world sales too.

Andy Dunn and Craig Elbert from the fashion retailer Bonobos.com graciously supplied their data to help us do this. Bonobos was founded in October 2007 as an online seller but now also sells merchandise at so-called Guideshops of its own and through a third party, the retailer Nordstrom. It's an ideal company for the purposes of our study, because all the items it sells have "touch and feel" attributes.

We focused on trying to understand whether: (1) first-time customers were getting information about Bonobos's products from existing customers in their real-world neighborhoods, and (2) social capital in the customers' real-world locations was affecting how information spread.

What we found was striking.[20]

Our analysis showed that up to half of all the first-time customers of Bonobos had gotten some helpful information about the company from existing customers of Bonobos who shared their offline neighborhood. Specifically, our model suggested that new customers were able to resolve some of their uncertainty about whether Bonobos's products were any good by interacting with other customers in their local neighborhoods.

Resolution of uncertainty was favorable to the seller—potential customers of Bonobos became convinced that the quality of Bonobos's products was higher than they may have initially guessed. Note that we didn't actually ask any customers about this directly—rather, this infer-

---

20 For more details, see Jae Young Lee and David R. Bell, "Neighborhood Social Capital and Social Learning for Experience Attributes of Products," *Marketing Science* 32, no. 6, (November–December 2013), 960–76.

ence is possible from the statistical modeling that we did on Bonobos .com sales data.

Now, what about the role of neighborhood social capital in this process?

Well, we split all the zip codes in our dataset into those with low social capital and those with high social capital, by utilizing survey responses in the Social Capital Community Benchmark Survey (SCCBS) collected by the Kennedy School at Harvard University.[21]

And we saw an interesting pattern. Bonobos.com sales were always higher in neighborhoods with more real-world social capital, i.e., in neighborhoods with more trust and interaction among neighbors.

Does this mean that social capital *causes* sales?

No, not directly.

When we undertook a more sophisticated modeling exercise, we realized the following: In neighborhoods with more social capital, *information transmission* is just better. What gets communicated has more veracity. If what is getting communicated is "good," as in, "These Bonobos pants are great!" then a seller benefits. That's what happened here. As we note in the original article, "Social capital *does not* operate on (sales) directly; rather, it improves the learning process and therefore indirectly drives sales when what is communicated is favorable."[22]

Finally, we wanted to do something that could potentially help the management team at Bonobos target new customers and new locations that would be most receptive to the company's products. Unfortunately, however, the SCCBS doesn't cover the entire United States, so it would be hard for us to make recommendations for locations where "true" social capital was not measured.

We needed to find some kind of proxy variable for social capital among the target customers—again, fashion-forward males, roughly ages twenty to forty-five—that was widely available.

This led to one of the more fun results in my academic research career. We found that the number of bars and liquor stores per capita in

21 The survey questions and the approach taken are laid out on p. 974–75 in Jae Young Lee and David R. Bell, "Neighborhood Social Capital and Social Learning for Experience Attributes of Products."
22 Ibid.

a zip code was a good proxy variable for social capital among the target group that we could use throughout the United States![23] Including this variable in our model showed that neighborhoods with more of this real-world feature had more efficient dissemination of information about Bonobos.com.

Since the information being conveyed turned out to be positive — i.e., our model implied that potential Bonobos customers formed a more favorable impression about the product after talking to existing customers — a *more efficient* transfer of information in high social capital locations in the real world led to faster growth in virtual-world sales. This implies that Internet sellers need to seed products and customers in markets where real-world trust and interaction are at a high level.

Big Media, Small Media, and Organic Growth for Sellers

I just showed how in the real world social capital moderates the flow of information in ways that help virtual-world sellers. Now, a related question concerns the extent to which "big" (national) and "small" (local) media help virtual-world sellers get started and eventually gain traction and succeed.

For some answers I turned to research conducted in Pittsburgh, at the University of Pittsburgh and Carnegie Mellon University.[24]

Big media like the *New York Times* and the *Washington Post* reside in big towns like New York City and Washington, DC. They have a large local base and a broad national following. Let's adopt the researchers' nomenclature and call these kinds of news services Traditional Media Outlets (TMOs).

In addition, there are more organic and typically smaller sources of information about products and services as well. These include re-

---

23 Of course it's not quite as good as the true social capital measure (we verified this in our article), but when the true measure isn't available, it makes sense to think a bit more broadly and creatively and look for a useful proxy measure.

24 Andrew T. Stephen and Jeff Galak, "The Effects of Traditional and Earned Social Media on Sales: A Study of a Microlending Marketplace," *Journal of Marketing Research* 69, no. 5 (October 2012), 624–39.

view sites and blogs and other forms of user-generated content (UGC). These are known as Social Media Outlets (SMOs).

So what's better for sellers? TMO coverage or SMO coverage?

To answer this question, the researchers collected data from the microfinance site Kiva.org. In its own words, Kiva is a site that enables users to "empower people around the world with a $25 loan." That is, any one of us could go there and lend $25. Each $25 loan is bundled into a larger loan (of say $500) for people like Yolanda in Peru, who wanted $750 to purchase construction materials.[25] The researchers wanted to know which of the two forms of media were more effective in generating sales and how the two interacted with each other (if at all). "Sales" in this instance were the number of microfinance loans offered at the site.

First, and perhaps not too surprising, TMOs provide the greater overall lift in sales for an online seller. They have a broader reach, and when an event like a media mention happens, sales spike. Places like the *New York Times* just have a lot of readers. SMO mentions (in local blogs and so on) also lift sales, but they have less *per event* effect. Perhaps this too is not that surprising. SMOs are smaller and more locally focused.

Now, on the other hand, individuals participating in SMOs are more committed to the issues and causes that define the SMO, so their engagement is stronger. That leads to a nice twist to the result: In *totality* SMOs were more effective for two reasons. First, even though the per-event (or mention) effect of being named and discussed in an SMO is smaller than the per-event effect of a mention in a TMO, the mentions are more frequent. Net-net, more frequent but smaller impacts add up to a greater total effect than large per-event, but infrequent mentions in major media.

And there is another benefit from SMOs as well. News bubbling up in SMOs tends to influence what is written in TMOs. In fact, the effect is very strong and statistically significant. Once you know it, it's understandable too. I mean if I worked for the *New York Times*, how would I come up with stories? I'd probably check out a few blogs to help me brainstorm ideas!

So in an indirect way what happens at SMOs can sometimes lead to TMO coverage, which in turn helps virtual-world sellers. This means

---

25 http://www.kiva.org/lend/615391.

that in the long run, the more "local" activity happening in SMOs among small but highly engaged user bases ends up being more beneficial to sellers.

Active and Passive Information Sharing

Researchers at NYU looked at a related question—whether one could build "viral features" into a product by having *individuals* rather than media outlets spread the news.[26] That is, could products be designed so that existing customers could facilitate organic sales growth for the seller?

The setting was an information application product set up on Facebook—the app allowed users to share information about movies, actors, and entertainment products.

Users were placed into one of three conditions. The first two were the experimental conditions. Whenever customers in the "passive-broadcast" condition used the product, messages were automatically sent to a random subset of individuals in their Facebook friend network. That is, they didn't have to do anything extra to send these messages, just use the product. Users in the "active-personalized" condition, on the other hand, were able to send invitations to others in their network and get them to try the product. The third condition was a control condition, in which neither of the previous two features was available.

Notice that users in the passive-broadcast condition had notifications randomly generated and distributed, and then displayed in the status bar of their friends' pages. The users themselves didn't have to do anything at all. Conversely, those with the active-personalized feature enabled could send a personalized invitation to their friends: "Hey Joe, try this out!"

So, which of the two features would "win" in terms of being better for the seller?

Well, let's dig a little to find out.

---

26 Sinan Aral and Dylan Walker, "Creating Social Contagion Through Viral Product Design: A Randomized Trial of Peer Influence in Networks," *Management Science* 57, no. 9 (September 2011), 1623–39.

The passive-broadcast feature requires absolutely no effort on the part of the user. It just activates automatically. It goes out to a wide and randomly selected group of friends, but without much of an active endorsement. The active-referral feature, on the other hand, requires a user to *select* particular friends as targets for the message (more about this word "selection" in a moment). This means that the user has to figure out which of her friends to target.

And, the winner is: passive broadcast.

Passive-broadcast messages are less effective on a *per user* basis, but they do hit a lot of people. Active referrals are more effective on a *per user* basis, but they hit fewer people, because it takes effort for the sender to figure out whom to target. So although they're more effective because recipients have been selected (targeted) and the referral message is personalized, they demand more effort from the referrer because she has to set up the referrals to start with.

So passive broadcast won out by a pretty large margin, increasing peer influence by a whopping 250 percent! Active referral wasn't too bad either, at a 100 percent lift. What this shows is that even though it is absolutely critical that sellers encourage their existing customers to target their friends and colleagues in the virtual world (and presumably the physical one too), this tactic doesn't always win out. Sometimes it's better to use the power of scale and automation to reach people passively, even if they are more dispersed and less well connected to the sender of information.

Side Note: Interactions with Selection and Treatment Effects[27]

Real- and virtual-world contagion and interaction are pervasive, so it's critical to understand the difference between selection and treatment effects in both environments.

I'll use another Diapers.com example to guide us through this.

First, the finding: Individuals who come into contact with a new

---

27 More jargon, but jargon that is insightful and good to know!

product or service as a result of direct word of mouth from others turn out to be better customers than those who arrive through other channels.[28] By "better," I mean that they are more loyal and have a higher customer lifetime value (CLV).

Why is this?

Well, first, they've been *selected* by a neighbor or by a friend. The referrer knows them and has an understanding of their needs and why the recommended product is a good fit for them. A *selection* effect, then, is what happens when an existing customer picks out another potential customer and shares information on a product or service.

Here's how it works: I happen to know that my neighbors John and Caroline have a newborn (I hear him quite a bit), so I tell them to try Diapers.com. They trust me, so they do. There's no way that either Marc or Vinnie, the cofounders of Diapers.com, could have this information. They don't know John or Caroline, let alone the fact that they have a new baby.

A *treatment* effect happens when someone who learned of a new product or service through word of mouth then speaks about it with others. Because John and Caroline were exposed to Diapers.com through social contagion and word of mouth (from me), they are more likely to pass on a similar recommendation to their friends and family than if they'd simply found Diapers.com directly, through, say, a Google search. This effect is quite subtle. But the takeaway is that when you learn about something through a social interaction, you're more likely to pass information along the same way.

Here's what we saw with the real Diapers.com data. A few years back, my coauthor Jeonghye and I looked at the first 100,000 customers acquired by Diapers.com. In particular, we checked who was referring new customers, how often, and how far and deep these "chains of referral" went. We found that the average customer had an 8 percent chance of referring others via word of mouth. On the other hand, a new cus-

---

28 A lot has been written about this. A nice recent example is Philipp Schmitt, Bernd Skiera, and Christophe Van den Bulte, "Why Customer Referrals Can Drive Stunning Profits," *Harvard Business Review* 89, no. 30 (June 2011). In it, the authors show that customers who opened accounts at a European bank as a result of referral had higher lifetime values than those who became customers through other routes.

tomer who came to Diapers.com through word of mouth had a 15 percent chance of doing so.[29]

Now, there are always some "special" people in any process. There are individuals who talk more, to more people, and with more enthusiasm and credibility than others.

Just to give you a sense of this, consider that while the average referring customer at Diapers.com recruits about three to four others, the best customers were bringing in as many as 150! Identifying these special people is no easy task, but it's very important to recognize that they exist and that they can be incredible advocates for a seller. When it comes to things that happen in the virtual world, it's always instructive for a seller to check out the *extreme* values of any statistic (number of customers referred, customers per zip code, product sales, etc.). The virtual world is tailor-made for extremes: that incredible customer who will refer hundreds of others, the video that is so compelling and convincing that millions will watch and share it, the deal that is so good that it will sell out in minutes.

So while the average values of these things are interesting, it's absolutely critical not only to understand the extremes, but also to create the potential for extreme things to happen. Also, there's usually systematic real-world influence on extreme behavior. In our analysis of Diapers .com data we also found that, on average, the best predictor of a customer's long-term value and their propensity for extreme levels of referral was their zip code location.

"Now-Casting" for Homes and Washing Machines Using Google Search

Now, people in different real-world locations don't have to be interacting explicitly for knowledge of what they're doing to be helpful to sellers. It could simply be that they're all doing their own thing but that in aggregate, the data they generate are useful for other purposes.

Here's a good example. The term "forecasting" is a familiar one. An

---

29 See also, Philipp Schmitt, Bernd Skiera, and Christophe Van den Bulte, "Referral Programs and Customer Value," *Journal of Marketing* 75, no. 1 (January 2011), 46–59.

analyst takes historical and current information—say home sales and average house prices for the last ten years in California—and predicts what they might be next year. This is not always that easy to do well, as Niels Bohr, the Nobel prize–winning Danish physicist, noted rather sardonically when he said, "It's difficult to make predictions, especially about the future."

Humorous and wildly incorrect predictions abound. Back in 1943, Thomas Watson, the CEO of IBM, famously said, "I think there is a world market for maybe five computers." One very good reason that predictions are so hard to make is that data inputs tend to be either dated or way too aggregated, or both.

However, research by academics at MIT and the University of Pennsylvania shows a possible and really incredible way out of this problem.[30] Enter the idea of "now-casting"—or, informally, the use of *real-time* information from the *virtual* world to produce both real- and virtual-world forecasts, sometimes of the future and sometimes also "forecasts" of what is going on right now.

According to some estimates, Google alone (which accounts for about two thirds of all search activity on the Internet) processes about 100 billion searches per month.[31] Imagine that some of those 100 billion odd searches were from people interested in buying new homes and entering terms like "Real Estate Agencies" and "Real Estate Listings" into Google.

When the researchers included counts of these virtual-world searches into their models, their ability to predict home prices and home sales in the *real* world improved dramatically. Intuitively, this makes sense. If more people are searching terms related to home purchasing today, then more purchases should be on the way tomorrow.

The researchers found that a 1 percent increase in search activity on the term "Real Estate Agencies" is associated with about 16,550 extra home sales for a quarter. How is that for clever? Our collective interest

30 Lynn Wu and Erik Brynjolfsson, "The Future of Prediction: How Google Searches Foreshadow Housing Prices and Sales" (working paper, the Wharton School, University of Pennsylvania, Philadelphia, 2013).

31 Dan Farber, "Google Search Scratches Its Brain 500 Million Times a Day," CNet, May 13, 2013, http://news.cnet.com/8301-1023_3-57584305-93/google-search-scratches-its-brain-500-million-times-a-day/.

in home buying right now, as expressed through virtual-world searches, says a lot about how much purchasing is going to take place in the real world tomorrow.

Now, while more searches about homes leads to more sales of homes, more sales of homes leads to more searches about other stuff. Stuff that goes into homes, for example. The same study showed that for each thousand homes sold in the *previous* quarter, there is a 1.14 percent increase in the virtual-world search index for household appliances sold today. While home sales are of huge importance to individuals and the economy overall, this is not the only case for which this method of prediction is accurate and of value. Armed with a bit of creativity and some technical skills, it's not that hard for someone to use Google Trends to track systematic patterns in things like searches for terms to do with health or for our favorite brands.[32]

Real-world consumers express their desires and needs individually in the virtual world, and this information becomes a powerful predictor for what happens in the real world in the future.

Product in Real World-Virtual World Landscape

Product, after information, is the second important commodity in the new topography of the real and virtual worlds. The tangible stuff that gets ordered, bought, and then ultimately shipped around.

THE LAST MILE AND THE FIRST AND LAST TOUCHES

One of the most challenging real-world issues for virtual-world sellers is the delivery of their goods (especially large and complicated things) to entities distributed over a large area, such as households and consumers. This challenge is one of the reasons that Webvan (the all-time greatest flame-out of Internet 1.0) failed, and it continues to be a key

---

32 For example, see the Google Flu Trends website at www.google.org/flutrends/about/how
.html.

issue for sellers of all stripes. In fact, the cost of shipping products, both financially and in terms of the thinking and logistics required, is a major impediment to the smooth flow of goods in the real world.

The Quidsi.com warehouse in Gouldsboro, Pennsylvania, ships about eighteen thousand orders a day to customers of Diapers.com, Soap .com, Wag.com, and the other members of the Quidsi family of sites. Now, while that's obviously a lot of stuff, perhaps more impressive is that the warehouse uses over twenty different box types and sizes. Each order is optimized with respect to the size of box and packing so as to make the shipment as economically efficient as possible.

So where are all those boxes going?

Well, they are going out into the real world, but *where* they go specifically has a lot to do with how all those customers were acquired in the first place. It turns out (as you might expect by now) that geography has a lot to do with that acquisition process.

The First Touch: Customer Aquisition and Location

The four main ways that most Internet retailers acquire customers are: (a) offline word of mouth (WOM), (b) online WOM, (c) traditional advertising, and (d) online search. Diapers.com is no different.

Orders go out all over the United States, but the way in which customers *come in* to Diapers.com varies a lot by real-world geography. Not every real-world location delivers virtual-world customers in exactly the same way. My colleagues at Yonsei University and Wharton and I built a statistical model and looked at customer locations for Diapers .com according to the *method* by which customers were acquired.[33]

While the number of potential target customers (families with babies) and their propensity to shop online varies a lot with geography, it turns out that the best ways of reaching and acquiring them does too. To illustrate this point, I'll focus on the most successful methods: offline WOM, magazine advertising, and online search. (Online WOM works

---

33 Jeonghye Choi, David R. Bell, and Leonard M. Lodish, "Traditional and IS-Enabled Customer Acquisition on the Internet," *Management Science* 58, no. 4 (April 2012), 754–69.

too, but just not as well as the other three in this case, for a key reason that I'll give shortly.)

All three of these methods generate roughly the same number of customers, but the geographic differences are startling. First, note that offline WOM is, by definition, an *interdependent* method of generating customers, because new customers are being brought to the seller by existing ones. WOM only exists through relationships.

So, where was offline WOM most successful?

Offline WOM was by far the most successful method of acquiring new customers for Diapers.com when three key conditions were present: when target customer density was high, when offline taxes on diapers were present, and when Diapers.com could ship products quickly (in one to two days). It turns out that target customer density (i.e., the number of households with babies per square mile) was a highly significant driver of acquisition through the other methods too, but the economic effect was much smaller.

What explains this?

First, target customer density drives offline WOM because it increases the chance that new and potential customers will interact or observe each other directly. In the article, we refer to this as a "social multiplier" enabled by real-world density. So, one very important thing is simply the density of potential customers in a location. Higher offline tax rates (which make online prices intrinsically more attractive) and fast shipping (greater convenience) are also critical, because these are two things that senders and recipients of WOM can actually *talk* about. Density puts people in contact, but for WOM to be enacted there has to be something to get the conversation going.

There's a related subtlety here too that I believe explains why offline WOM can be so much more effective than its online counterpart.

Imagine that you and I live in the same physical location and that I'm a customer of Diapers.com. If I tell you that Diapers.com is great because it's got one-day delivery and the prices are amazing, this information is highly relevant to you.

Why?

Since you and I live in the *same location*, that means we will get exactly the *same benefits* from an Internet seller and also face the same offline alternatives. In short, there would be "benefit-matching" between the sender and the recipient of WOM, and that will make the WOM more compelling. My great experience is also available to you!

If, however, you live thousands of miles away, then you might have quite a different experience. Perhaps in your city there are no taxes on offline purchases and the delivery time from the online seller in question would be two to three days. You still like and trust me just the same (that's good!) but the WOM I am giving you is not going to be as compelling because your *real-world circumstances* are very different than mine.

This idea of "benefit matching" goes a long way toward explaining why we found online WOM to be a weaker form of WOM overall. If WOM is being shared online and if senders and recipients are in different locations (which is quite likely when WOM travels the virtual world), then there's a very good chance that "benefit matching" may not occur, whereas with offline WOM, it *always* does.

Magazine advertising turned out to be very effective for picking up customers in more rural and spread-out locations, where there was less opportunity for incidental interaction among customers. So advertising is going to be especially useful in real-world locations where customers are less likely to come into contact with a good number of other people.

Online search delivers customers in a fairly predictable way. The number of new customers generated through this channel is approximately proportional to the population in a location. The larger the location, the more customers arriving through the search funnel.

Running From the (Tax) Man

Death. And Taxes.

We will avoid the former (in this discussion at least) but spend a bit of time looking at research on the latter, as it's one of the most contentious and interesting aspects of the evolving topography. Offline sales taxes have been around for as long as anyone can remember, and in some states in the United States they can reach up to 9 percent. Until very recently, most online sellers in the United States could avoid collecting and remitting them (as I noted in chapter 2, RESISTANCE). The "loophole" was that only virtual-world sellers with a real-world presence were required to collect taxes. In fact, Thomas Stemberg, the founder of the large retailer Staples, said this in a letter to the US Congress:[34]

> It is illogical and now patently unfair that Staples.com is required to collect and remit sales taxes because of our local commitment when many other dot.com competitors do not have a similar requirement.

While this quote indicates the predicament previously faced by real-world US sellers, the effect of sales taxes on buyer behavior is also very large. Austan Goolsbee, a former economic adviser to President Barack Obama, calculated that if sales taxes were to be levied on virtual-world sales at the average rate prevailing on the real world (about 8 percent) then demand online would fall by up to 20 percent.[35]

That is a very big effect! So, even though the landscape is changing to require all virtual-world sellers to collect sales taxes, it's still vitally important to understand how their presence or absence affects shopping behavior and competition among sellers.

A clever study by researchers at MIT and Northwestern University dug into exactly how the presence of taxes in the real world, but not in the virtual one, affects the behavior of shoppers and sellers alike. Specifically, the researchers took advantage of a "natural experiment," wherein a mostly virtual-world retailer who previously did not have a real-world store in a state that levies sales taxes decided to open one.

So imagine a burgeoning retailer had no store in California, but then decided to open one in San Francisco. As of July 2013, the tax rate would be 8.75 percent. Now, because the seller has a *real-world presence* in San Francisco, that means it will have to collect an additional 8.75 percent on *all* orders placed at its *virtual-world store* and shipped in the state of California.

The effect of this shift on incentives for both shoppers and sellers is profound.

In chapter 2 (RESISTANCE) we examined the reverse problem: virtual-world sellers facing competition from real-world stores' mov-

34 Thomas Stemberg (2005), "Staples Letter of Support for S. 2152."
35 Austan Goolsbee, "In a World Without Borders: The Impact of Taxes on Internet Commerce," *Quarterly Journal of Economics* 115, no. 2 (May 2000), 561–76.

ing in on their territory. I showed that virtual-world sellers lose sales in a particular location after a real-world seller moves in (think back to what happens to Amazon.com sales in a location after a physical book-seller opens a store there). This loss occurs because the real-world store starts to eat into the local trading area of the virtual-world seller.

Following the California example, if a physical bookshop opens a store in the zip code CA 94105 in San Francisco, then Amazon.com sales will fall *in that location*. Bookworms who live in CA 94105 can now shop in a real store right in their location, and that hurts sales at Amazon.com. Of course, we would not expect the introduction of a store in CA 94105 (San Francisco) to affect Amazon.com sales way down in other parts of the state such as in CA 90210.

However, the effects of imposing sales tax collection on the virtual-world seller are far greater and more widespread. When a *virtual-world* seller opens a *real-world store* and becomes responsible for collecting taxes on all sales in an *entire state*, the researchers found that sales at the website go down across the *entire state* by more than 11 percent. So even customers who are unable to visit the store in San Francisco (and can-nibalize Internet sales that way) are put off from buying on the website because of the 8.75 percent "price increase" (due to the tax).

Buyers are clearly put off by taxes.

And what of sellers?

Well, the researchers found that multichannel retailers with stores and sites doing a lot of business over the web are *less* likely to open new real-world stores in states with high sales taxes.

Buyers and sellers alike, run from taxes!

Goods and Information, Brands and Commodities

As the topography of real-world/virtual-world interaction evolves, it's natural that sellers who began life in one world need to acquire presence in the other. This extension—of virtual-world sellers into the real world, and vice versa—has important implications for customer behavior.

Toni Moreno from Kellogg and Santiago Gallino from Tuck and I examined what happens when a virtual-world seller, in this case the eyewear retailer WarbyParker.com, expands into the real world and opens showrooms.[36] Eyewear is a category with a significant "touch and feel" component since generally people want to try on glasses before buying them. We found that the introduction of a physical "inventory showroom" in a location, i.e., a complete display of all Warby Parker products within another store, had three interesting effects on demand for Warby Parker products *at that location*.

First, overall sales increased. This is perhaps not surprising as there was now a showroom where none previously existed; more interesting, an expansion into real-world presence increase led to an increase in *virtual-world sales at that location*. The presence of a physical store conferred awareness and credibility benefits to the brand, such that more people were inclined to buy on the site.

Second, the conversion rate on the Home Try-On program, where customers could receive five frames delivered to their homes for free for five days, increased in locations near the showroom. The availability of a showroom provided the best alternative for the most "risk averse" customers who wanted to really touch and feel products before buying. Previously, these customers would likely have ordered a Home Try-On, but now that these customers were diverted to the new channel, those that remained in the Home Try-On option had a higher propensity to buy. Further confirmation of this was seen in the reduction of return rates for online sales. Third, visits to the website by potential customers located in the vicinity of the real-world showroom increased.

So, the evolving topography facilitates the development of new business models in which the real- and virtual-world operations of sellers support each other in unique ways. It is well known that online retailers, for example, derive significant cost advantages from centralized management and fulfillment of inventory. Conversely, they are disadvantaged when it comes to giving customers a rich experience to sample their products. So, a virtual-world seller (like WarbyParker.com) can benefit significantly by combining centralized fulfillment with real-world product sampling.

This highlights an important difference between virtual-world sell-

---

36 David R. Bell, Santiago Gallino, and Antonio Moreno, "Inventory Showrooms and Customer Migration in Omni-Channel Retail: The Effect of Product Information" (working paper, Kellogg School of Management, Northwestern University, Evanston, Illinois, 2013).

ers that control the manufacturing, distribution, and branding of their own products—companies like Bonobos.com and WarbyParker.com—and those, like Amazon, that sell commodities (brands built by others). When the former advance into the real world, they should prioritize the *informational* dimension of their businesses, giving customers more opportunity to touch, feel, and experience their products. Sellers like Amazon, however, should prioritize *fulfillment*, improving the speed at which customers can access products. Products like Amazon Locker and Amazon Drone are of course designed to do exactly that.[37]

Summary

"If you can't beat 'em, join 'em" goes the popular saying. Since the real and virtual worlds compete with *and* complement each other, the next logical step is to weave them together. In delivering either product or information, where one is weaker, the other is stronger. If you're a virtual-world seller of "touch and feel" products, you need real-world touch points with customers.

Real-world engagement and virtual-world reach go hand in hand. Smart sellers create rich local experiences and let their customers amplify and share them online. Sellers that win have the best products *and* the richest narratives. Because their products are great, their customers actively refer (and customers from referral are almost always more valuable). Since the narrative is rich, the story evolves and keeps getting told. Traditional media mentions give "bumps" and social media outlets keep priming the pump. These tightly organized and locally based sites do more for the overall growth of virtual-world sellers. Conversations are more frequent and targeted, and these sites sometimes originate stories in traditional media too.

Today's searches are tomorrow's purchases, because when shoppers reach out in the virtual world, they reveal intent. When they reach out to *each other*, their conversations are more powerful when they share local circumstances and derive the same benefits from sellers. When

---

37 http://www.cbsnews.com/news/amazon-unveils-futuristic-plan-delivery-by-drone/.

sellers reach out, most shoppers want to be known, within limits. Virtual world advertising is more effective when obtrusive or contextually targeted, but not both.

Finally, the fixed Internet dramatically reduces search and geographic frictions, but the mobile Internet brings them back. On mobile we want *more seamless* information (i.e., we are less tolerant of search friction) and we're *more attracted* to options that are locally close (i.e., we are less willing to travel). So, we're becoming simultaneously more spontaneous and more local in our behaviors. And this will create huge opportunities and enhancements for all local commerce. Your real-world life, made better by the virtual one.

No longer "either/or," just a single transforming topography—you'll succeed when you use one world to enhance what you do in the other.

YOU

Making GRAVITY Work for You

L ima, Peru, is a city with extremely little rainfall, averaging only around an inch a year in the coastal part of the city and not much more than that in the inland area. This puts considerable pressure on its water supply. Even though rain is rare, humidity can run close to 100 percent in the mornings, given the city's proximity to the Pacific Ocean.

So when professors in Lima wanted to showcase the engineering talent at the University of Engineering and Technology of Peru (UTEC), they built a billboard that could turn air into water.[1] (Sadly, there was no subsequent transformation of that liquid into wine.) A short video on YouTube explains how the billboard works and shows it in action. More than three quarters of a million people around the world have watched the clip.

At Ohio State University, Dr. Christopher Kaeding donned Google Glass while performing surgery so that he could stream real-time point-of-view video from the operating room and consult with other col-

---

[1] Matt Peckham, "Finally, a Billboard That Creates Drinkable Water Out of Thin Air," *Time*, Tech, March 5, 2013, http://techland.time.com/2013/03/05/finally-a-billboard-that-creates-drinkable-water-out-of-thin-air/.

leagues in distant locations.[2] This allows him to get more input on his work and leads to tremendous benefits for the patient as well.

In early 2012, the photographer John Butterill founded Virtual Photo Walks,[3] and in February of that year he took the hospital-bound Corey Fisk (who'd had MS for ten years) on a "virtual photo walk" through the woods. This idea has sparked amateur and professional photographers around the world to perform similar treks. When the shoots take place, viewers from all over tune in and watch the proceedings via Google Hangout.[4]

As these endeavors suggest, increasingly we "hunger for experiences that join the real and digital worlds together," as Kim Snow, Google's New York City–based creative director, so nicely puts it.[5] That really speaks to the thesis of this book—the two worlds are tightly linked and our behaviors in each are mutually reinforcing.

As long as we keep living in the real world (for the most part), I think it makes sense to think of it as the *foundation*. We might think of the virtual world, on the other hand, as the *amplifier*. Any situation or circumstance experienced in the real world can be shared and made better in, or by, the virtual one.

So how can you make sense of all of this and apply it in your own context?

Well, we've been on a journey that started with some basic and surprising facts about the real world and the way it's organized (chapter 1, GEOGRAPHY) and ended with the new and emerging landscape, where the real and virtual worlds are intertwined (chapter 6, TOPOGRAPHY). We also covered a lot of ground in between.

Now, where to from here?

I'm hoping that the academic research that underlies this book and the ideas we've shared through the GRAVITY framework will help you

2   http://www.gizmag.com/google-glass-streaming-surgery/28867/.

3   Butterill's website is www.virtualphotowalks.org. For the story about Corey Fisk, see Jessica Lum, "Virtual Photo Walks Make Photography Accessible to People with Disabilities," PetaPixel, March 5, 2012, http://petapixel.com/2012/03/05/virtual-photo-walks-make-photography-accessible-to-people-with-disabilities/.

4   For an example, see "John Butterill's Virtual Photo Walks," YouTube, August 6, 2012, www.youtube.com/watch?v=y1Uv7as5ZmI.

5   "Seminar on Possibilities," remarks given at the Google Brand Health Summit, September 19, 2013.

navigate and appreciate how the real and virtual worlds interact and where that interaction is headed.

I'm also hoping that you'll be motivated to do something, whether it's investing time and energy in a friend's or family member's idea, or getting something going yourself. The good news is that it's never been easier to start something. As the famous Kiwi (Sir) Edmund Hillary once said: "You don't have to be a hero to accomplish great things — to compete. You can just be an ordinary chap, sufficiently motivated to reach challenging goals."[6]

One way to see the framework in action is through the lens (upcoming pun intended) of an example that provides a good view of it. There are many lenses, many examples, but I wanted to share a story with which I am quite familiar and that I find very motivating.

Once again, this story suggests that location is, indeed, (still) everything.

A Story of Friendship and Vision — in the Real and Virtual Worlds

FOUR FRIENDS MEET IN THE REAL WORLD

Back in the summer of 2008, four soon-to-be fast friends, Neil Blumenthal, Dave Gilboa, Andy Hunt, and Jeff Raider, arrived at Wharton to begin business school. Dave had just returned from a vacation and had left his Olivier People's glasses on the plane. They would cost over $500 to replace.

Neil and Dave discussed the situation, and ended up with the following question: "Why should a pair of glasses cost more than an iPhone?" The answer is quite complex and not our direct concern here, but it has to do with the fact that large monopolies control the production, marketing, and distribution of eyewear in the United States, leading to a rather unfortunate situation for consumers. In short, the friends con-

---

6   Edmund Hillary, *High Adventure: The True Story of the First Ascent of Everest* (New York: Oxford University Press, 1955).

cluded, the system for delivering eyewear and eye care in the real world was broken. And they were going to use the virtual world to fix it.

Neil in particular knew quite a bit about what was going on. Through his role as a director of a nonprofit providing glasses in developing countries, he'd learned about the enormous gap between manufacturing costs and retail prices in the developed world.[7] He, Dave, Andy, and Jeff hatched a plan to sell eyewear online.

That's right: they decided to sell *prescription eyewear online.*

If you haven't heard of Warby Parker before, perhaps you're having a reaction that's similar to the one I had when the guys first sat in my office and explained what they were doing. Even though I don't wear glasses myself, I was pretty sure that people liked to actually hold them in their hands and try them on before buying, so I was somewhat skeptical that what the team was planning to do could, in fact, be done.

That was then.

This is now.

A lot has happened since those early days in February 2010 (when the business was launched). So far the team has sold over half a million pairs of glasses, and in the spring of 2013, Warby Parker opened a flagship store in the real-world location of SoHo, Manhattan. Warby has also partnered with other real-world retailers, and the team members have driven a retrofitted "class trip" school bus across the United States to advertise their wares. So, let's view what they've done (and, by analogy, what you could do too), through the GRAVITY framework.

THE *GRAVITY* FRAMEWORK IN ACTION

GEOGRAPHY

The real-world circumstances of customers vary tremendously across a large country like the United States and indeed across most other coun-

---

7   Christopher Marquis and Laura Velez Villa, "Warby Parker: Vision of a 'Good' Fashion Brand," Harvard Business Press case study 9-413-051, Harvard Business School, July 25, 2012.

tries as well. In starting the business, the Warby Parker team thought it made sense to begin where (real-world) markets are large—places like the northeast of the United States—and would likely be receptive to the new business. Some customers would have "decent" offline options; others would not. (I say "decent" because in most instances US consumers have pretty poor choices in this product category). Some locations might require showrooms in the future; others would not.

Recall from chapter 1 that there is a positive correlation between virtual-world buying in a particular real-world location and the number of virtual-world sellers located there. This makes sense—in places where people are receptive to virtual-world solutions for their personal consumption, there are likely to be more virtual-world employers.

So if you are trying to get a virtual-world business going, it makes sense to choose a real-world location carefully—one where, on average, customers and employees are co-located. Many forward-thinking e-commerce companies, such as Warby Parker and Bonobos, create open environments at corporate headquarters where customers can visit.

Step one in applying the GRAVITY framework is to understand the implications of GEOGRAPHY, particularly in terms of *access to early customers and employees.*

RESISTANCE

The second step for the team at Warby Parker was to figure out how they would eliminate or least mitigate the two key frictions—search and geographic—that customers encounter in the real world. So, they implemented a Home Try-On program, enabling potential customers to receive five pairs of glasses (without lenses) for free, and have five days to try them on.[8] This means that customers do not need to "travel to the store" to overcome uncertainty about the product—the product comes to them instead.

Thus, the sampling program dramatically reduced "geographic friction"; wherever they were located, customers could receive the product. More than this, the Home Try-On program eliminated an important

---

8   For more information, see www.warbyparker.com/home-try-on.

friction that is particular to many virtual-world sellers. When customers can't touch and feel the product before buying it, this can be a significant barrier to an online purchase. The Home Try-On program eliminates this friction.

Transparency in pricing and the reduction of search friction around low prices was accomplished through a standard $95 price point that was also communicated in terms of margin. That is, the site shows current and potential customers the price and margin relationships for typical competitors, as well as for Warby Parker itself.

Thus, step two is about countering RESISTANCE to information search and purchase by giving customers the means to reduce their uncertainty. Specifically, it's about giving customers *access to the information required to enable them to make better choices and feel comfortable doing so.*

ADJACENCY

Locating first in the best market(s) and focusing on them while systematically eliminating frictions are both necessary conditions, but they alone are hardly sufficient to ensure success.

Acting decisively and correctly in relation to what GEOGRAPHY and RESISTANCE imply for you will get you started in the right direction, but it won't be enough to get you to where you ultimately need to be.

Internet businesses compete everywhere and have customers everywhere, so in order for any new business or idea to expand beyond the introduction phase, it's absolutely critical to leverage the power of ADJACENCY.

How does Warby Parker do this?

The Home Try-On program is one important tool to this effect. It gets product into the hands of consumers who have expressed an interest in at least trying it. Customers who are receptive to the brand (but not yet committed to buying) can easily sample the products. Also, and more important, the program gets the product out there, meaning that more than just the prospective customer will be exposed to it. Market research shows that customers who request a Home Try-On packet share the contents with another three to four people on average. This means that *even when* customers who get the product *don't* end up ultimately buying it, there is still a positive spillover of information about the brand to adjacent others (friends, colleagues, family members, and so on).

My own econometric analysis corroborates this as well—sampling by nonbuyers has a statistically significant effect on the amount of information being spread to adjacent others. I have yet to formally test this, but my hunch is that the size of the effect is largest when Home Try-On boxes are delivered to offices rather than homes as well.

Why is this?

Remember our earlier example of Soap.com (with those brightly colored boxes that I get delivered to my office)? Like me, you probably have more office colleagues than you do family members, so a delivery to the office is likely to be seen and experienced by many people.

Warby Parker also leverages adjacency effects in real-world locations—by putting showrooms in places where potential customers are going to be not only the most receptive to the brand, but also most likely to tell others about the product.

So step three is all about understanding how to reach that vital second layer of customers—those beyond the immediate core. And even more important, it's about recognizing that in locations where there is one customer who is interested in what you are doing, there will, thanks to homophily, be many *proximate others* who will be interested too!

You want to make sure that you give potential customers the ability to share your product or service and therefore *grant access to a proximate group that will then deliver more customers for you.*

VICINITY

Warby Parker leverages and acts on the important concept of VICINITY by understanding that real-world communities separated by great distances often contain similar types of customers.

In line with the prescriptions of GEOGRAPHY and RESISTANCE, and after the company first opened offices and showrooms in New York (its offices served simultaneously as showrooms), their showroom strategy covered places like Oklahoma City, Nashville, and Richmond, in addition to Chicago and Los Angeles. This expansion strategy recognizes two critical points.

First, it recognizes that although the smaller destinations are quite some distance apart, they share characteristics that make them equally attractive. Locations that exhibit similarity in dimensions of demographics and access to stores will be filled with customers who have similar tendencies to buy from Warby Parker.

Second, the strategy recognizes that while demand from larger centers is invaluable for initial growth and customer seeding—e.g., the business is very much anchored in New York and to some extent Boston and Los Angeles—it cannot grow and thrive without demand from the numerous smaller areas that together make up the Spatial Long Tail introduced in chapter 4.

That is, in order to be the truly dominant force in the industry that the founding team hope Warby Parker will be, they will need to gather demand from small locations scattered throughout the United States (and ultimately the world) that share characteristics and are therefore in the same vicinity (from a marketplace perspective).

So as a general principle, you need to make sure you have a strategy that allows you to link and *access clusters of customers who are distant from each other yet belong in the same marketplace—yours.*

ISOLATION

Every Internet business I've looked at, from Diapers.com to Bonobos.com to Warby Parker, benefits tremendously from a clear understanding of what ISOLATION means for it.

Remember, your isolated customers are absolutely your best friends and advocates for three good reasons.

First, the real world has been especially "unkind" to them in the sense that it is dismissive of their needs and preferences. They've been crowded out by local others who don't share their tastes. Second, and as a direct result of the first point, these customers have a high propensity to seek liberation in the virtual world. And third, they are among the most vocal in their praise (as the Warby Parker Facebook page attests!) and are among the least price sensitive.

So make sure that you identify the real-world locations that will give you *access to the most receptive customers: those most starved of local choices that are relevant to them.*

TOPOGRAPHY

While there are undoubtedly other businesses that understand this point too, it's hard to think of a seller that does a better job than Warby Parker at navigating the real-world/virtual-world landscape and conceiving of it as one integrated TOPOGRAPHY.

Warby Parker reaches customers in both worlds and also does things in the real world that get picked up and amplified in the virtual one. Here are my two favorite examples (among many) of the latter practice.

Back in September 2011, when the business was still in its relative infancy, fashion week rolled around in New York, as it does every year. The company wanted to somehow make a splash, but as a new start-up it didn't have much ready cash lying around. Nevertheless, the team needed to do something that was (1) consistent with their brand identity, (2) going to be "high impact" and seen by a large audience, and (3) cheap to execute.

A difficult trifecta to achieve even under the best of circumstances!

The brand identity of Warby Parker comes from the names of two fictitious characters, Zagg Parker and Warby Pepper, who are featured in an unpublished Jack Kerouac manuscript.[9] As an iconic American author who personifies a certain kind of countercultural cool, Kerouac is a nice fit for an American brand looking to appeal to a young, hip audience. But more than this, the fact that he is a writer plays into the notion of books and libraries, which, with a bit of narrative, can segue to eyewear.

Anyway, it just so turned out that during Fashion Week that year the New York Public Library was exhibiting unpublished works by Kerouac,

---

9   As told on the Warby Parker website: www.warbyparker.com/history.

including one that contained the characters that inspired the Warby Parker name. The team decided that it would be brand relevant, high impact, and low cost (and of course fun!) to have friends and models slowly take over a floor of the New York Public Library one day in the midst of Fashion Week.

The result: A crowd of friends and models lounged in the library, looking erudite while buried in their books. Words like "Jensen" and "Begley" emblazoned on the visible spines and covers of the books were the names of Warby Parker frames and the "readers" were wearing those very frames! As you might imagine, this scene resonated with many of those in the target market and received a good deal of press coverage.[10]

So, this real-world event was reported, shared, amplified, and commented on through a variety of virtual-world sources.

The second example took place a few months later. In early 2012 the team decided to retrofit an old yellow school bus (a familiar, iconic vehicle of sorts), and drive it all over the country. And so began the Warby Parker Class Trip.[11]

This was essentially a movable real-world showroom journeying all over the country, including places that did not have Warby Parker stores or third-party retailers that stocked Warby Parker glasses. In addition to experiencing the Trip when it rolled into town, customers could share the journey virtually and chat about it via Twitter, Instagram, and a variety of other virtual-world platforms. Customers also had the opportunity to enter a contest involving the virtual-world sharing of these real-world activities.[12]

My colleagues Toni and Santiago and I collected and analyzed data on the locations where the bus stopped. In all of these locations, we found significant increases in *online* sales, in addition to the sales that took place on the bus itself.[13]

---

10 See, for example, Patricia Garcia, "Warby Parker Takes Over the New York Public Library," *Vogue Daily*, September 7, 2011, www.vogue.com/vogue-daily/article/warby-parker-takes-over-the-new-york-public-library/#1.

11 As related on the Warby Parker website, www.warbyparkerclasstrip.com/.

12 http://www.warbyparkerclasstrip.com/2013/08/21/whereswarby-artifactuprising-instagram-contest/.

13 David R. Bell, Santiago Gallino, and Antonio Moreno, "Inventory Showrooms and Customer Migration in Omni-Channel Retail: The Effect of Product Information" (working paper, Kellogg School of Management, Northwestern University, Evanston, Illinois, 2013).

The upshot of this model for your own entrepreneurial efforts? Make sure that you allow your customers to *access your business in both real-world and virtual-world contexts in one seamless and natural experience.*

You and Your Team

If you think about Warby Parker, you'll see that the founders began with an idea that *personally resonated* with them. So as you go about your daily life searching, shopping, and selling, ask yourself the following question: "What's wrong with the status quo?"

To paraphrase my friend Kirsten Green, managing partner of Forerunner Ventures (and an investor in Warby Parker as well), there are three absolute must-haves for those embarking on a new venture.

First, you should ideally be addressing a very common problem — one that affects a large market. Second, the founders of your team — and most research shows that two (or more) is better than one — should exhibit magnetic personalities, with a passion for the company that is obvious and infectious. These qualities will inspire others to come on board and see the vision through to fruition. Third, and this is nonnegotiable, the team must be able to efficiently and effectively get things done. Ideas are a dime a dozen. Successful execution of them is something else.

BACK TO THE START

"Oh, take me back to the start," sings Chris Martin in "The Scientist," crooning about a lover. While what I have to say here is not quite as romantic, I do appreciate the sentiment. So, let's go there — and reiterate three key ideas infused throughout the book and central to the successful application of GRAVITY:

- Always keep in mind that the *benefits* of shopping, selling, and searching online cannot be separated from the locations where customers live in the real world. This means that you must take into account the cities and towns that potential customers reside in, whom they choose to live among, and what they have access to.

- Your virtual-world business, whether selling goods, services, or information, must quickly create *sufficient density*—often by connecting and aggregating individuals from disparate locations. Density breeds critical mass and engagement, and is necessary for more density to follow.
- Remember that the *tactics and strategies* required for gaining followers, disseminating content, or selling products online need to be customized for different locations. Moreover, the virtual world is a great amplifier for whatever gets done locally in the real one.

AHEAD TO THE FUTURE

Only you can know what it is that you want to pursue to use the virtual world to improve what happens in the real one. Nevertheless, it will most likely come from one of the following four domains. Each area probably warrants a book in its own right . . . but that's a topic for another day. For now I'll just attempt to encapsulate the basic ideas. Your budding solution to a problem might

1. *Disrupt an Existing Value Chain.* The problem you identify might be a "broken" market (like the US market for eyewear), in which customers are exploited by a business ecosystem that protects very high margins for the seller.
2. *Democratize Access to Goods and Services.* In many markets (education and entertainment, for example) access to content is restricted—there's not sufficient capacity for everyone to get an MBA from the Wharton School, for example, and only so many people can attend a musical concert at a certain time and place. Effective use of technology—think of Coursera, for one—is changing the game.
3. *Pool Resources and Improve Utilization.* Most privately owned automobiles sit idle for up to twenty-two or more hours per day, and rooms in many homes go unused. Businesses like Zipcar, RelayRides, and Airbnb attack these problems, but there are plenty of other avenues to explore as well. Many assets are duplicated when sharing is in fact more efficient.

4. *Create a Better Match Between Supply and Demand.* There are countless instances in which excess capacity exists but never gets married off to unmet demand. This is especially true for services, and that's why businesses like Uber.com ("Everyone's private driver") and TaskRabbit.com ("Your to-do's, done") have taken off.

The Last Word

I feel fortunate to live in a time when the real world has never been richer and more colorful, and when the virtual world amplifies and enhances it daily. To you, the reader, my heartfelt thanks. I hope that this book has helped you to better understand and appreciate how the real and virtual worlds interact. I wish you well as, now armed with the knowledge of GRAVITY, you navigate your own journey, perhaps all the way to creating a "Warby Parker" of your own!

ACKNOWLEDGMENTS

I am extraordinarily grateful to all the friends and colleagues who have helped me with this book. Thank you for the ideas, inspiration, critique, and, most of all, the encouragement to bring this book to life.

A few people warrant special thanks.

First, my close friend Olivier Ledoit, a truly exceptional scholar from the University of Zurich and Alpha Crest Capital, told me to write this book.

Dave Moldawer (formerly at Amazon, now at creativeLIVE) believed in the thesis of the book and signed me to Amazon. Carly Hoffmann and Katie Salisbury at Amazon guided me through the publishing process and were always gracious with deadlines, even when I slipped. Polly Rosenwaike worked tirelessly on the manuscript, reworking it from start to finish several times. Jill Westfall did an exceptional round of edits as well.

Toni Moreno from Northwestern University provided extensive and detailed feedback. Maggie Lee, in particular, provided invaluable critiques as well. Daniel Corsten from IE Business School and Tom Forte from TAG Advisory Group in New York sharpened the writing, and Mike Gibbons at Wharton helped drive marketing.

Most of what I've learned about research and writing is due to my adviser Jim Lattin at Stanford and my friend Christophe Van den Bulte at Wharton. I'm indebted to my coauthors on the core research that anchors the book: Jeonghye Choi (Yonsei University), Sam Hui (New York University), Jae Young Lee (Yonsei University), Len Lodish (Wharton), and Sangyoung Song (Ewha University).

My own research was made possible only because of the incredible generosity of start-up founders and executives who shared their data, time, and insights. These are the people who really make things happen: Ari Sabah (Netgrocer.com); Marc Lore, Vinnie Bharara, and Scott Hilton (Quidsi.com); Neil Blumenthal, Dave Gilboa, Andy Hunt, Jeff Raider, and Erin Collins (WarbyParker.com); and Andy Dunn and Craig Elbert (Bonobos.com).

I am extremely grateful to my friends who graciously came and spoke in my very first digital marketing and e-commerce classes at Wharton | Philadelphia and Wharton | San Francisco. I've learned a ton from you guys: Pooja Batra (@iampoojabatra), Joe Cohen (@josephcohen), Mike Cohen (Birchbox.com), Rob Coneybeer (Shasta Ventures), Craig Elbert (Bonobos.com), Kirsten Green (Forerunner Ventures), Mitchell Green and Nimay Metha (Lead Edge Capital), Dr. John Johnston (Jon M. Huntsman School of Business, Utah State), Lawrence Lenihan (Firstmark Capital), David Hauslaib (@davidhauslaib) and Tom Balamaci (@tbalamaci), Andy Katz-Mayfield and Jeff Raider (Harrys .com), Aileen Lee (Cowboy Ventures), Phil Migliarese (@JiuJitsumatrix), and Jennifer Yen (Purlisse.com).

Finally, I'm deeply grateful for the privilege of being a faculty member at Wharton. My colleagues in the marketing department are a special group, and I learn from them every day. It's been wonderful to get to know so many exceptional Wharton undergraduate and MBA students over the years too. Special thanks goes to Joe Cohen and Chloe Heckman for their feedback on early drafts.

BIBLIOGRAPHY

Agrawal, Ajay and Avi Goldfarb (2008), "Restructuring Research: Communication Costs and the Democratization of University Innovation," *American Economic Review* 98 (4), 1578–90.

Albuquerque, Paulo, Bart J. Bronnenberg, and Charles Corbett (2007), "A Spatio-Temporal Analysis of Global Diffusion of ISO 9000 and ISO 14000 Certification," *Management Science* 53 (3), 451–68.

Allison, Ralph I. and Kenneth P. Uhl (1964), "Influence of Beer Brand Identification on Taste Perception," *Journal of Marketing Research,* 1 (3), 36–39.

Anderson, Chris (2006), *The Long Tail: Why the Future of Business is Selling Less of More* (New York: Hyperion).

Anderson, Eric T., Nathan M. Fong, Duncan I. Simester, and Catherine E. Tucker (2010), "How Sales Taxes Affect Customer and Firm Behavior: The Role of Search on the Internet," *Journal of Marketing Research* 47 (2), 229–39.

Aral, Sinal and D. Walker (2011), "Creating Social Contagion Through Viral Product Design: A Randomized Trial of Peer Influence in Networks," *Management Science* 57 (9), 1623–39.

Barr, Alistair (2013), "Feature: From the Ashes of Webvan, Amazon Builds a Grocery Business," Reuters, June 16, 2013, http://in.reuters .com/article/2013/06/16/amazon-webvan-idINDEE95F04H201 30616.

Bell, David R. and Randolph E. Bucklin (1999), "The Role of Internal Reference Points in the Category Purchase Decision," *Journal of Consumer Research* 26 (2), 128–143.

Bell, David R. and Sangyoung Song (2007), "Neighborhood Effects and

Trial on the Internet: Evidence from Online Grocery Retailing," *Quantitative Marketing and Economics* 5 (4), 361–400.

Bell, David R., Santiago Gallino, and Toni Moreno (2013), "Inventory Showrooms and Customer Migration in Omni-Channel Retail: The Effect of Product Information," (working paper, Kellogg School of Management, Northwestern University, Evanston, Illinois).

Blum, Bernado and Avi Goldfarb (2006), "Does the Internet Defy the Law of Gravity?," *Journal of International Economics* 70 (2), 384–405.

Boorstin, Julia (2013), "Why and How the 'Breaking Bad' Finale Broke Records," CNBC September 30, 2013, www.cnbc.com/id/1010 74132.

Box, George E. P. and N. R. Draper, (1987), *Empirical Model Building and Response Surfaces* (New York: John Wiley & Sons).

Bronnenberg, Bart, Sanjay Dhar, and Jean-Pierre Dube (2009), "Brand History, Geography, and the Persistence of Brand Shares," *Journal of Political Economy* 117 (1), 87–115.

Bronnenberg, Bart, Jean-Piere Dube, and Matt Gentzkow (2012), "The Evolution of Brand Preferences: Evidence from Consumer Migration," *American Economic Review* 102 (6), 2472–2508.

Bronnenberg, Bart and Carl F. Mela (2004), "Market Roll-Out and Retailer Adoption of New Brands," *Marketing Science* 23 (4), 500–518.

Brynjolfsson, Erik, Jeffrey Hu, and Mohammed S. Rahman (2009), "Battle of the Retail Channels: How Product Selection and Geography Drive Cross-Channel Competition," *Management Science* 55 (11), 1755–65.

Brynjolfsson, Erik, Jeffrey Hu, and Duncan Simester (2011), "Goodbye Pareto Principle, Hello Long Tail: The Effect of Search Costs on the Concentration of Product Sales," *Management Science* 57 (8), 1373–86.

Brynjolfsson, Erik, Jeffrey Hu, and Michael Smith (2003), "Consumer Surplus in the Digital Economy: Estimating the Value of Increased Product Variety at Online Booksellers," *Management Science* 49 (1), 1580–96.

Cain Miller, Claire and Stephanie Clifford (2013), "To Catch Up, Walmart Moves to Amazon Turf," *New York Times*, October 19, 2013, www.nytimes.com/2013/10/20/technology/to-catch-up-walmart-moves-to-amazon-turf.html?_r=0

Cairncross, Frances C. (1997), *The Death of Distance: How the Communications Revolution is Changing our Lives* (Boston: Harvard Business School Press).

Carlson, Nicholas (2012), "The Man Made $28,000 a Month Writing Fake Book Reviews Online," *Business Insider*, August 27, 2012, www.businessinsider.com/this-guy-made-28000-a-month-writing-fake-book-reviews-online-2012-8.

Cha, M., H. Haddadi, F. Benevenuto, and K. Gummadi (2010), "Measuring User Influence in Twitter: The Million Follower Fallacy," Association for the Advancement of Artificial Intelligence, www.aaai.org/home.html.

Chen, Yuxin, James Hess, Ronald Wilcox, and John Zhang (1999), "Accounting Profits Versus Marketing Profits: A Relevant Metric for Category Management," *Marketing Science* 18 (3), 208–29.

Chevalier, Judith and Dina Mayzlin (2006), "The Effect of Word of Mouth on Sales: Online Book Reviews," *Journal of Marketing Research* 43 (3), 345–54.

Choi, Jeonghye, and David R. Bell (2011), "Preference Minorities and the Internet," *Journal of Marketing Research* 58 (4), 670–82.

Choi, Jeonghye, David R. Bell, and Leonard L. Lodish (2012), "Traditional and IS-Enabled Customer Acquisition on the Internet," *Management Science* 58 (4), 754–69.

Choi, Jeonghye, Sam. K. Hui, and David R. Bell (2010), "Spatiotemporal Analysis of Imitation Behavior Across New Buyers at an Online Grocery Retailer," *Journal of Marketing Research* 47 (1), 75–89.

Dewan, Shaila (2013), "As Renters Move In, Some Homeowners Fret," *New York Times*, August 28, 2013, www.nytimes.com/2013/08/29/business/economy/as-renters-move-in-and-neighborhoods-change-homeowners-grumble.html.

Dickson, E. J. (2013), "The New York Times Can't Stop Trolling Philadelphia," *Salon*, June 13, 2013, www.salon.com/2013/06/13/the_new_york_times_cant_stop_trolling_philadelphia/.

Dishman, Lydia (2013), "Three Reasons Why Mickey Drexler Can Help Scale Warby Parker," *Forbes*, September 18, 2013, www.forbes

.com/sites/lydiadishman/2013/09/18/three-reasons-why-mickey-drexler-can-help-scale-warby-parker/.

Farber, Dan (2013), "Google Search Scratches Its Brain 500 Million Times a Day," CNet, May 13, 2013, http://news.cnet.com/8301-1023_3-5758 4305-93/google-search-scratches-its-brain-500-million-times-a-day/.

Florida, Richard (2005), "The World is Spiky: Globalization Has Changed the Economic Playing Field But Hasn't Leveled It," *Atlantic Monthly* (October), 48–51.

Forman, Chris, Anindya Ghose, and Avi Goldfarb (2008), "Examining the Relationship Between Reviews and Sales: The Role of Reviewer Identity Disclosure in Electronic Markets," *Information Systems Research* 19 (3), 291–313.

Forman, Chris, Anindya Ghose, and Avi Goldfarb (2009), "Competition between Local and Electronic Markets: How the Benefit of Buying Online Depends on Where You Live," *Management Science* 55 (1), 47–57.

Garcia, Particia (2011), "Warby Parker Takes Over the New York Public Library," *Vogue*, www.vogue.com/vogue-daily/article/warby-parker-takes-over-the-new-york-public-library/#1.

George, Lisa and Joel Waldfogel (2003), "Who Affects Whom in Daily Newspaper Markets," *Journal of Political Economy* 111 (4), 765–84.

Ghose, Anindya, Avi Goldfarb, and Sang Pil Han (2013), "How Is the Mobile Internet Different? Search Costs and Local Activities," *Information Systems Research* 24 (3), 613–31.

Glaeser, Edward L. (2010), "A Tale of Many Cities," *New York Times*, Economix, April 20, 2010, http://economix.blogs.nytimes.com/2010/04/20/a-tale-of-many-cities/.

Godes, David and Dina Mayzlin (2004), "Using Online Conversations to Study Word-of-Mouth Communications," *Marketing Science* 23 (4), 545–60.

Goldfarb, Avi and Catherine E. Tucker (2011), "Online Display Advertising: Targeting and Obtrusiveness," *Marketing Science* 30 (3), 389–404.

—— (2012), "Search Engine Advertising: Channel Substitution When Pricing Ads to Context," *Management Science* 57 (3), 458–70.

Goolsbee, Austan (2000), "In a World Without Borders: The Impact of

Taxes on Internet Commerce," *Quarterly Journal of Economics* 115 (2), 561–76.

Goolsbee, Austan and Peter C. Klenow (2002), "Evidence of Learning and Network Externalities in the Diffusion of Home Computers," *Journal of Law and Economics* 45 (2), 317–43.

Harris, Jessica (2013), "From Scratch: Marc Lore and Vinnie Bharara, Founders of Diapers.com," interview, National Public Radio, September 19, 2013, www.npr.org/2013/09/18/223785364/marc-lore-and-vinnie-bharara-founders-of-diapers-com.

Hilber, Christian A. L. (2010), "New Housing Supply and the Dilution of Social Capital," *Journal of Urban Economics* 67 (3), 419–37.

Hillary, Edmund (1955), *High Adventure: The True Story of the First Ascent of Everest* (New York: Oxford University Press).

Hitsch, Gunter, Ali Hortacsu, and Dan Ariely (2010), "What Makes You Click?—Mate Preferences in Online Dating" (working paper, University of Chicago, Chicago, Illinois).

Hortacsu, Ali, Asis Martinez-Jerez, and Jason Douglas (2009), "The Geography of Trade in Online Transactions: Evidence from eBay and MercadoLibre," *American Economics Journal: Microeconomics* 1 (1), 53–74.

"Indiana's Peculiar Liquor Laws May Drive You To Drink," *Indiana Star*, editorial, May 18, 2013, www.indystar.com/article/20130518/OPINION08/305180019/.

Iyengar, Raghu, Christophe Van den Bulte, and Jae Young Lee (2013), "Social Contagion in New Product Trial and Repeat" (working paper, Wharton School, University of Pennsylvania, Philadelphia, Pennsylvania).

Jefferies, Duncan (2013), "Is Technology and the Internet Reducing Pupils' Attention Spans?," *Guardian*, March 11, 2013, www.theguardian.com/teacher-network/teacher-blog/2013/mar/11/technology-internet-pupil-attention-teaching.

Katz, E. and P. Lazarsfeld (1955), *Personal Influence* (Glencoe, IL: Free Press).

Lee, Jae Young and David R. Bell (2013), "Neighborhood Social Capital and Social Learning for Experience Attributes of Products," *Marketing Science* 32 (6), 960–76.

Libai, Barak, Eitan Muller, and Renna Peres (2005), "The Role of Seeding in Multi-Market Entry," *International Journal of Research in Marketing* 22 (4), 375–93.

Lieber, Ethan and Chad Syverson (2011), "Online Versus Offline Competition" in *The Oxford Handbook of the Digital Economy*, ed. Martin Peitz and Joel Waldfogel (New York: Oxford University Press,), 189–223.

Loewenstein, George F. (1988), "Frames of Mind in Intertemporal Choice," *Management Science* 34 (2), 200–214.

Lum, Jessica (2012), "Virtual Photo Walks Make Photography Accessible to People with Disabilities," PetaPixel, March 5, 2012, http://petapixel.com/2012/03/05/virtual-photo-walks-make-photography-accessible-to-people-with-disabilities/.

Mackle, Robert (2013), "Ohio State Doctor Shows Promise of Google Glass in Live Surgery," Ohio State University Wexner Medical Center, August 27, 2013, www.medicalcenter.osu.edu/mediaroom/releases/Pages/Ohio-State-Doctor-Shows-Promise-of-Google-Glass-in-Live-Surgery.aspx.

Marquis, Christopher and Laura Velez Villa (2012), "Warby Parker: Vision of a 'Good' Fashion Brand," Harvard Business School Press, case 413–051.

Martokso, David (2013), "Barack Obama is Political King of Fake Twitter Followers, With More Than 19.5 MILLION Online Fans Who Don't Really Exist," *Daily Mail*, September 24, 2013, www.dailymail.co.uk/news/article-2430875/Barack-Obama-19-5m-fake-Twitter-followers.html.

Mayzlin, Dina, Yaniv Dover, and Judith Chevalier (2014), "Promotional Reviews: An Empirical Investigation of Online Review Manipulation" *American Economic Review* (forthcoming).

Molloy, Raven, Christopher L. Smith, and Abigail Wozniak (2011), "Internal Migration in the United States," *Journal of Economic Perspectives* 25 (3), 173–96.

Oberholzer Gee, Felix and Joel Waldfogel (2009), "Media Markets and Localism: Does Local News En Español Boost Hispanic Voter Turnout?," *American Economic Review* 99 (5), 2120–28.

Oyen, O. and M. L. De Fleur (1953), "The Spatial Diffusion of an Airborne Leaflet Message," *American Journal of Sociology* 59 (2), 144–49.

Peckman, Matt (2013), "Finally a Billboard That Creates Drinkable

Water Out of Thin Air," *Time*, March 5, 2013, http://techland.time
.com/2013/03/05/finally-a-billboard-that-creates-drinkable-
water-out-of-thin-air/.

Pelissie du Rausas, Matthieu, James Manyika, Eric Hazan, Jacques
Bughin, Michael Chui, and Remi Said (2011), "Internet Matters:
The Net's Sweeping Impact on Growth, Jobs, and Prosperity,"
McKinsey Global Institute.

"The Philly Legal Eagles, Rizio, Hamilton & Kane, P.C., Debuting New
Billboard Location On I-95 May 13th," press release, PRWeb, May
9, 2013, http://www.prweb.com/releases/prweb2013/5/prweb1071
6174.htm.

Putman, Robert D. (2000), *Bowling Alone: The Collapse and Revival of
American Community* (New York: Simon & Schuster).

Schmitt, Philipp, Bernd Skiera, and Christophe Van den Bulte (2011),
"Referral Programs and Customer Value," *Journal of Marketing* 75
(1), 46–59

—— (2011), "Why Customer Referrals Can Drive Stunning Profits,"
Harvard Business Review 89 (6), 30.

Shriver, S., Harikesh Nair, and R. Hofstetter (2013), "Social Ties and
User-Generated Content: Evidence from an Online Social Network," *Management Science* 59 (6), 1425–43.

Sinai, Todd and Joel Waldfogel (2004), "Geography and the Internet:
Is the Internet a Substitute or Complement for Cities?," *Journal of
Urban Economics* 56 (1), 56–74.

Skiera, Bernd and Nadia Abou Nabou (2013), "PROSAD: A Bidding
Decision Support System for Profit Optimizing Search Engine
Advertising," *Marketing Science* 32 (2), 213–20.

Stemberg, Tom (2005), "Staples Letter of Support for S. 2152."

Stigler, George J. (1961), "The Economics of Information," *The Journal
of Political Economy* 69 (3), 213–25.

Streifeld, David (2012), "Giving Mom's Book Five Stars? Amazon May
Cull Your Review," *New York Times*, December 22, 2012, www.ny
times.com/2012/12/23/technology/amazon-book-reviews-deleted-
in-a-purge-aimed-at-manipulation.html.

Strogatz, Steven (2009), "Math and the City," *New York Times*, Opinionator, http://opinionator.blogs.nytimes.com/2009/05/19/math-
and-the-city/.

Sun, Monic, Xiaoquan Zhang, and Feng Zhu (2013), "To Belong or Be Different? Evidence from a Large-Scale Field Experiment in China" (working paper, Marshall School of Business, University of Southern California, Los Angeles, California).

Tang, Christopher, David R. Bell, and Teck-Hua Ho (2001), "Store Choice and Shopping Behavior: How Price Format Works," *California Management Review* 43 (2), 56–74.

Tiebout, Charles (1956), "A Pure Theory of Local Expenditures," *Journal of Political Economy* 64 (5), 416–24.

Toubia, Olivier, and Andrew T. Stephen (2013), "Intrinsic vs. Image-Related Utility in Social Media: Why Do People Contribute Content to Twitter?," *Marketing Science* 32 (3), 368–92.

Trusov, Michael, Anand V. Bodapati, and Randolph E. Bucklin (2010), "Determining Influential Users in Internet Social Networks," *Journal of Marketing Research* 47 (4), 643–58.

Tucker, Catherine E. (2011), "Social Advertising" (working paper, Sloan School of Management, Massachussets Institute of Technology, Cambridge, Massachusetts).

United States Census Bureau, "E-Stats," United States Department of Commerce, Economics and Statistics Administration, May 27, 2010, www.census.gov//econ/estats/2008/2008reportfinal.pdf.

Van Alstyne, Marshall and Erik Brynjolfsson (2005), "Global Village or Cyber-Balkans? Modeling and Measuring the Integration of Electronic Communities," *Management Science* 51 (6), 851–68.

Van der Laan, Joost W., "Online Grocery Retailing Is a Tricky Business," RetailEconomics, http://retaileconomics.com/online-grocery-retailing/.

Volpe, Mike (2013), "10 Horrific Stats About Display Advertising," Hubspot, April 29, 2013, http://blog.hubspot.com/marketing/horrifying-display-advertising-stats.

Waldfogel, Joel (2003), "Preference Externalities: An Empirical Study of Who Benefits Whom in Differentiated-Product Markets," *RAND Journal of Economics* 34 (3), 557–68.

—— (2007), *The Tyranny of the Market: Why You Can't Always Get What You Want* (Boston: Harvard University Press).

Wasserman, Todd (2012), "10 Insanely Clickable Banner Ads," Mashable, May 28, 2012, http://mashable.com/2012/05/28/10-insanely-clickable-banner-ads/.

Wauters, Robin (2010), "Confirmed: Amazon Spends $545m on Diapers.com Parent Quidsi," TechCrunch, November 8, 2010, http://techcrunch.com/2010/11/08/confirmed-amazon-spends-545-million-on-diapers-com-parent-quidsi.

Whyte, William H. Jr. (1954), "The Web of Word of Mouth," *Fortune* 50 (November), 140–43.

Wu, Lynn and Eric Brynjolfsson (2013), "The Future of Prediction: How Google Searches Foreshadow Housing Prices and Sales" (working paper, Wharton School, University of Pennsylvania, Philadelphia, Pennsylvania).

Yang, Sha and Greg M. Allenby (2003), "Modeling Interdependent Consumer Preferences," *Journal of Marketing Research* 40 (3), 282–94.

Yildirim, Pinar, Esther Gal-Or, and T. Geylani (2013), "User Generated Content and Bias in News Media," *Management Science* 59 (12), 2655–66.

Zettelmeyer, Florian, Fiona Scott Morton, and Jorge Silva-Risso (2003), "Consumer Information and Discrimination: Does the Internet Affect the Pricing of New Cars to Women and Minorities?," *Quantitative Marketing and Economics* 1 (1), 65–92.

ABOUT THE AUTHOR

David R. Bell is the Xinmei Zhang and Yongge Dai Professor at the Wharton School, University of Pennsylvania. An award-winning scholar and teacher, David developed Wharton's first course on digital marketing and electronic commerce. He holds a PhD from the Graduate School of Business at Stanford University and is an active angel investor in several digital marketing and e-commerce start-ups. David lives in Philadelphia and San Francisco, but he remains a citizen of his native home, New Zealand, and a fan of all things Kiwi.

INDEX